Richmond

Jake Hughes

Student's BOOK

CB078499

A1

Keep it REAL!

Contents

S

VOCABULARY People

I can talk about people in my life.

1 S0.1 **Match the words in the boxes with the pictures. Listen, check and repeat.**

animal boy classmates friends girl man parents student teacher woman

1

2

3

4

5

6

7

8

9

10

2 S0.2 **Read and listen. Match the dialogues with the pictures.**

1

Lucas: Hi. I'm Lucas. I'm a new student.
Leo: Hi, Lucas. This is Miss Tims. She's your teacher.
Lucas: Hello, Miss Tims.
Miss Tims: Hi, Lucas. We're in Class 2. Come with me.
Lucas: OK.

2

Miss Tims: This is Lucas. He's a new boy in the class.
Class: Hello, Lucas!
Miss Tims: These are your classmates. They're very friendly!
Lucas: Hi, everyone.
Miss Tims: This is your desk. It's next to Linda.

3

Lucas: Hi, Linda.
Linda: Hi. You're Lucas Sánchez!
Lucas: That's right. How do you know?
Linda: My parents and your parents are friends!
Lucas: Wow ... and now we're classmates!

a

b

c

3 **Read the dialogues again. Choose the correct answers. Copy the sentences in your notebook.**

1 *Leo* / *Lucas* is a student.
2 Lucas is a *boy* / *girl*.
3 *Linda* / *Miss Tims* is a teacher.
4 Miss Tims is a *man* / *woman*.
5 Lucas and Linda are *friends* / *classmates*.

4 **Work in pairs. Make sentences about the people in your life.**

1 ... and ... are classmates.
2 ... is a teacher.
3 ... is a student.
4 ... and ... are my friends.
5 ... and ... are my parents.

GRAMMAR Subject pronouns

I can use subject pronouns.

1 **Match the subject pronouns in the box with the pictures.**

he I it she they we you (x2)

2 **In your notebook, rewrite the sentences with the subject pronouns in the box.**

~~he~~ it she they we

1 **Lucas** is a student. *He is a student.*
2 **Lucas and I** are classmates.
3 **Carol and Tony** are my parents.
4 **Linda** is in my class.
5 **The bag** is on the desk.

be: affirmative

I can use the verb *be* in the affirmative.

3 **Read the grammar box. Complete the rules with the short forms of *be*.**

Singular		Plural	
I'm (I **am**)	from Mexico.	We**'re** (We **are**)	friends.
You**'re** (You **are**)	in my class.	You**'re** (You **are**)	in Class 3.
He**'s** (He **is**)	a teacher.	They**'re** (They **are**)	my parents.
She**'s** (She **is**)	a student.		
It**'s** (It **is**)	a cat.		

Rules

We can use *be* in the long form or the short form after subject pronouns.

Long form	*am*	*is*	*are*
Short form	[1] ...	[2] ...	[3] ...

4 S0.3 **Copy and complete the sentences with the short form of *be*. Listen, check and repeat.**

1 He ... my friend.
2 They ... my classmates.
3 She ... a teacher.
4 You ... twelve.
5 I ... a student.
6 It ... my book.
7 We ... in English class.
8 They ... my parents.

5 S0.4 **Choose the correct answers. Copy the text in your notebook. Listen and check.**

Hi, my name's Laura and I [1]*'re / 'm* twelve. I [2]*'m / 's* a student at Redwood High School. This is Sally. She [3]*'s / 'm* eleven and she [4]*'re / 's* my friend. We [5]*'s / 're* in Class 1. Today we [6]*'re / 'm* in English class. The English teacher [7]*is / am* Mr Mason. He [8]*'re / 's* really friendly! My classmates [9]*is / are* really happy. English [10]*is / am* fun!

6 **Work in pairs. Make sentences with the words in the box.**

I my classmates my friend my parents the teacher we you

I'm a student.

FAST FINISHER

Write a profile about you like in Exercise 5.

Hi, my name's ...

VOCABULARY The alphabet

I can spell words.

1 S0.5 **Listen and repeat the letters.**

2 **Say the letters in each group. Notice how they have the same sound as the words in bold.**

play	A, H, J, K,
me	B, C, D, E, G, P, T, V
yes	F, L, M, N, S, X, Z
my	I, Y
no	O
you	Q, U, W
are	R

3 S0.6 **Listen and spell the names in your notebook.**

What's your name?

My name's ...

1 My name's *Kathy*.
2 My name's ...
3 My name's ...
4 My name's ...

4 **Work in pairs. Ask and answer the questions from Exercise 3.**

A: What's your name?
B: My name's Enrique.
A: How do you spell that?
B: E-N-R-I-Q-U-E.

Numbers

I can use numbers.

5 S0.7 **Listen and repeat the numbers.**

6 **PRONUNCIATION Numbers**

S0.8 **Listen and repeat the numbers.**

1 a thir<u>teen</u> b <u>thir</u>ty
2 a four<u>teen</u> b <u>for</u>ty

7 S0.9 **Listen and write the numbers you hear in your notebook.**

1	a	15	b	50		3	a	16	b	60
2	a	17	b	70		4	a	19	b	90

8 **Work in pairs. Say the numbers.**

9 **Work in pairs. Write a number in your notebook. Can your partner say the number?**

10 S0.10 **Listen to the dialogues. Write the answers in your notebook.**

What's your name?

What's your surname?

How old are you?

What's your phone number?

11 **Work in pairs. Ask and answer the questions in Exercise 10.**

GRAMMAR Demonstrative pronouns

I can use demonstrative pronouns.

1 **Look at the pictures in the grammar box. Complete the rules.**

Singular	**This** is a bag.	**That** is a window.
Plural	**These** are pens.	**Those** are books.

Rules

We use *this* and *these* for things that [1]*are / aren't* near us.

We use *that* and *those* for things that [2]*are / aren't* near us.

2 SO.11 **Match the questions with the answers. Listen and check.**

1 What's this?
2 What's that?
3 What are those?
4 What are these?

a They're keys.

b They're shoes.

c It's a phone.

d It's a guitar.

3 **Work in pairs. Practise the dialogues in Exercise 2.**

4 **Work in pairs. Ask and answer questions about things in the classroom.**

A: What's this?
B: It's a book.
A: What are those?
B: They're coats.

VOCABULARY Colours

I can talk about colours.

5 SO.12 **In your notebooks, match the words in the box with the colours. Listen, check and repeat. What is your favourite colour?**

black blue brown green grey
orange pink red white yellow

6 **Work in pairs. Say the colours of the objects.**

A: It's black.
B: They're blue.

7 **Work in pairs. Point to something in the classroom. Ask and answer questions about the colour.**

A: What colour is this/that?
B: It's pink.

8 **Work in pairs. Ask and answer *What colour is your ...?* with the things in the box.**

bag bedroom bike car notebook phone

FAST FINISHER

Write sentences about the colour of things in your home.

My sofa is blue.

READING

I can find information in a text.

1 S0.13 **Read and listen to the profiles. Match them to the people.**

Home · Board · Contact

Tell us about you!

1 Hello. I'm George and I'm eleven years old. I'm from Dallas in the USA. Adam is my best friend. We're in Class 2 at North Dallas High School. My favourite colour? Um … I have two: blue and white! They're the colours of my favourite football team, the Dallas Cowboys!

2 Hi. My name's Katie. I'm twelve. I'm from Manchester in the UK. My favourite colour is yellow. My phone is yellow, my bag is yellow, my bedroom is yellow … everything is yellow! My best friend is Amy and she's twelve, too. We're at Salford Secondary School together.

2 **Read the text again. Find the information and complete the table in your notebook.**

	1	2
Name:	…	…
Age:	…	…
City:	…	…
School:	…	…
Best friend:	…	…
Favourite colour(s):	…	…

SPEAKING Classroom language

I can ask questions and follow instructions in class.

3 S0.14 **Listen and read. Match the pictures with the dialogues.**

1 **Teacher:** What's wrong?
Student: I don't understand.
2 **Student:** How do you say 'bom dia' in English?
Teacher: Good morning.
3 **Student:** What does 'family' mean?
Teacher: Your mum, dad, brothers, sisters …
4 **Student:** Can you repeat that, please?
Teacher: Welcome.
5 **Student:** How do you spell that?
Teacher: W-E-L-C-O-M-E.
6 **Teacher:** It's 9.15!
Student: Sorry I'm late.

4 S0.15 **Listen and repeat the Useful language.**

Useful language

Classroom language

I don't understand.
How do you say ... in English?
What does ... mean?
Can you repeat that, please?
How do you spell that?
Sorry I'm late.

5 **Copy and complete the dialogue with your own ideas.**

Student: How do you say '...' in English?
Teacher: '...'
Student: How do you spell that?
Teacher: '...'

6 **Work in pairs. Practise your dialogues.**

FAST FINISHER

Write a dialogue between a teacher and a student.

School life

1

Vocabulary: Classroom objects; Adjectives | **Grammar:** Articles; Plural nouns; *be*: affirmative and negative | **Speaking:** Talking about timetables | **Writing:** A student profile

VOCABULARY Classroom objects

I can talk about things in the classroom.

1 1.1 **Match the words in the box with the pictures. Listen, check and repeat.**

board chair computer desk door headphones laptop pen pencil pencil case rubber ruler shelf smartphone tablet window

2 **Copy the table in your notebook. Complete it with the objects from Exercise 1.**

Things in a pencil case	
Parts of a classroom	
Technology	

3 **Work in pairs. Point at the picture and ask and answer questions.**

A: What's this/that?

B: It's a desk.

4 **With a partner, say the things you see in your classroom.**

It's a chair.

Now watch the vlog.

FAST FINISHER

Write a list of classroom objects that you also have in your bedroom.

door, window, desk ...

LS Language summary: Unit 1 SB p.118

This is my bag

READING **I can** match descriptions with pictures.

WHAT'S IN YOUR BAG?

Bags are important. We carry everything we need for the day in our bags. Today we ask three people from Burnham High School, 'What's in your bag?'

1

Hi, what's your name?

My name's Lorna.

What's in your bag, Lorna?

This is a Science book and these are lunch boxes. I have two. My sandwiches are in this box, and an apple and an orange are in that box. And this is a pencil case with one, two, three pencils, a rubber and a ruler.

2

Hello, what's your name?

I'm Mrs Johnson. I'm a teacher.

What's in your bag?

OK, let's see. This is a pencil case. And in the pencil case … pens. They're black, blue and red. And what are these? They're books. These are two dictionaries. An English dictionary and a French dictionary. And this is a laptop and this is a smartphone.

3

And what's your name?

Fabian.

OK, Fabian, what's in your bag?

These are my books … a Maths book, an Art book, a notebook. What's this? Oh yes, it's an umbrella. And this is a pencil case – with pens and pencils. And this is an apple and my smartphone. Oh, and finally these are headphones.

a

b

c

1 **Look at the pictures of the bags. What can you see in them?**

pencil case, ruler…

2 1.2 **Read and listen to the text. Match the bags with the people.**

1 Lorna … 2 Mrs Johnson … 3 Fabian …

3 **Copy the table in your notebook. Read the text again and tick (✓) the things in the bags.**

	books	technology	food
Lorna	✓		
Mrs Johnson			
Fabian			

4 **Work in pairs. Ask and answer the question from the text.**

A: What's in your bag?

B: This is a pencil case …

5 **Word Power** **Find five school subjects in the text and write them in your notebook. Which is your favourite subject?**

Science, …

6 **THINK CRITICALLY** **In some schools, students use their smartphones in the classroom. Is this a good idea or a bad idea? Think of one good thing and one bad thing.**

I think it's a good idea because …

I think it's a bad idea because …

GRAMMAR Articles

I can use articles before nouns.

Now watch the grammar animation.

1 1.3 **Read the grammar box. Copy the words with the correct articles in your notebooks. Listen, check and repeat.**

Use *an* before nouns that begin with vowels (*a, e, i, o, u*).
an *apple* ***an*** *umbrella*
Use *a* before nouns that begin with consonants.
a teacher **a** book

1 orange

2 watch

3 pen

4 ice cream

Plural nouns

I can use singular and plural nouns.

2 1.4 **Read the grammar box. Write the plurals of the words in the pictures in your notebooks with the correct numbers. Listen, check and repeat.**

	Singular	Plural
Most nouns	a pen	pen**s**
Nouns ending in -*ch*, -*s*, -*sh*, -*x*, -*z*	a box	box**es**
Nouns ending in -*f*, -*fe*	a shelf	shel**ves**
Nouns ending in consonant + -*y*	a dictionary	dictionar**ies**

1 a sandwich

two sandwiches

2 an umbrella

3 a dress

4 a baby

5 a book

6 a leaf

3 Read the Look! box. Match the singular nouns with the irregular plural nouns.

Look! Irregular plural nouns

Some plural nouns don't end in -*s*.

1 a person	a children
2 a child	b men
3 a woman	c people
4 a man	d women

4 Work in pairs. What can you see in the picture? Use the nouns in the box with articles or numbers.

~~apple~~ board child clock desk laptop pen rubber ruler shelf smartphone tablet umbrella ~~window~~ woman

an apple, two windows ...

FAST FINISHER

Write about the things in your classroom. Use numbers or articles.

a dictionary, six pens ...

LS Language summary: Unit 1 SB p.118

This isn't difficult!

VOCABULARY and LISTENING Adjectives

I can listen for detail.

1 1.5 **Match the pictures with the adjectives. Listen, check and repeat.**

beautiful big boring cheap difficult
easy expensive happy interesting old
sad short small tall ugly young

1

2

3

4

5

6

7

8

Look! **Adjective order**

Adjectives come before nouns:
This is a ***big classroom.***
Adjectives come after *be:*
This classroom *is* ***big.***

2 **Read the Look! box. In your notebook, put the words in the correct order to make sentences.**

1 is / tall / father / my
2 men / the / old / are
3 young / are / children / those
4 lessons / are / English / easy
5 a / subject / difficult / is / that
6 am / I / person / a / happy
7 computers / expensive / these / are
8 an / interesting / is / book / this

3 1.6 **Listen to a dialogue between two friends, Liam and Ava. Match them to their Maths classes.**

4 1.6 **Listen again. Are the sentences true (T) or false (F)?**

1 Liam is happy.
2 Maths is difficult.
3 Liam's Maths lessons are boring.
4 Ava's Maths lessons are interesting.
5 Ava uses tablets in Maths lessons.
6 Today is Friday.

LS Language summary: Unit 1 SB p.118

GRAMMAR *be*: affirmative and negative

I can use *be* in the affirmative and negative.

Now watch the grammar animation.

1 **Read the grammar box. Copy and complete the rule with the long form of *be*.**

	Affirmative	Negative
I	I'**m** a teacher.	I'**m not** a student.
you	You'**re** happy.	You **aren't** sad.
he	He'**s** at home.	He **isn't** at school.
she	She'**s** tall.	She **isn't** short.
it	It'**s** cheap.	It **isn't** expensive.
we	We'**re** in this class.	We **aren't** in Class 3.
they	They'**re** from the UK.	They **aren't** from Brazil.

Rule

We can use *be* in the long form or the short form after subject pronouns.

Long form	1 …	2 …	3 …	4 …	5 …	6 …
Short form	'm	's	're	'm not	aren't	isn't

2 1.7 **Choose the correct answers to complete the start of Ava and Liam's dialogue. Listen and check.**

Ava: Hi, Liam. How are you?
Liam: Oh, I 1 *'m not / aren't* bad.
Ava: Uh-oh, you 2 *'re / aren't* happy. What's wrong?
Liam: It's my Maths lessons. They 3 *'re / 's* difficult.
Ava: Well, Maths 4 *aren't / isn't* easy. What's the teacher like?
Liam: She 5 *'s / isn't* OK, but the lessons … they 6 *aren't / 're* boring.
Ava: Boring? Maths lessons 7 *am not / aren't* boring. They 8 *'re / aren't* fun!

3 PRONUNCIATION Negative contractions

1.8 **Listen and repeat.**

1 **isn't** He isn't happy.
2 **aren't** They aren't cheap.

4 **Copy and complete the sentences with the affirmative (+) or negative (–) form of *be*.**

1 Today … Saturday. (–)
2 I … happy today. (+)
3 The students … at school. (–)
4 This smartphone … cheap. (+)
5 You … my teacher. (–)
6 English lessons … interesting. (+)
7 I … tall. (–)
8 My school … big. (+)

5 **Work in pairs. Make affirmative and negative sentences about the pictures.**

That's an ugly building. It isn't beautiful.

6 **Work in pairs. Write three true sentences and three false sentences about you. Can your partner guess if the sentences are true or false?**

A: I'm happy today.
B: True.
A: I'm thirteen.
B: False! You aren't thirteen. You're twelve.

FAST FINISHER

Write three affirmative and three negative sentences about your classmates.

Jorge isn't tall …

LS Language summary: Unit 1 SB p.118

KEEP TALKING!

Time for class!

READING and LISTENING

I can understand a school timetable.

1 Look at the pictures. Which school subjects can you see?

2 Read the school timetable for Monday and Tuesday. Write the day and time of each lesson (a–d).

a

Day: ______
Time: ______

b

Day: ______
Time: ______

c

Day: ______
Time: ______

d

Day: ______
Time: ______

		9.00–10.15	10.15–10.45	10.45–12.00	12.00–1.00	1.00–2.30	2.45–4.00
MONDAY	Lesson: Classroom: Teacher:	**English** B14 Mrs Jones	**BREAK**	**Spanish** C3 Sra García	**LUNCH**	**Art** A6 Mr Ashton	**P.E.** Gym Mr Sansom
TUESDAY	Lesson: Classroom: Teacher:	**Maths** C3 Mr Norton	**BREAK**	**History** A12 Ms Foster	**LUNCH**	**Science** B2 Ms Hancock	**English** B14 Mrs Jones

FRIDAY	Lesson: Classroom: Teacher:	1 ... 2 ... Mr Garrett	**BREAK**	3 ... B4 Mme 4 ...	**LUNCH**	5 ... A3 Mr 6 ...	7 ... 8 ... Mrs Davis

3 Read the timetable again and answer the questions.

1 Which subject is on Monday and on Tuesday?
2 Which classroom has two different lessons?
3 What time is break?
4 Which two lessons are 1.5 hours?

4 Which day do you prefer: Monday or Tuesday? Why?

5 FIND OUT Students in the UK learn Maths, Science, Art, P.E., History, English and other languages. Find two more British school subjects.

6 1.9 **Listen to a teacher talk about the timetable for Friday. Which of the lessons in the box do the students have?**

Art	English	French	History
Music	P.E.	Science	Spanish

7 1.9 **Listen again. Copy and complete the timetable for Friday.**

SPEAKING Talking about timetables

I can say the days of the week and tell the time.

1 1.10 **Listen and read. What is the problem?**

Jake: What day is it today?
Sarah: It's Wednesday.
Jake: Science is on Wednesday. What time is it?
Sarah: It's five to nine.
Jake: Oh no!
Sarah: What?
Jake: The Science lesson is at nine o'clock. We're late!

2 1.11 **Listen and repeat the days of the week.**

3 **Work in pairs. Ask and answer the questions.**

1 What day is it today?
2 What day it is tomorrow?
3 What days are the weekend?

4 1.12 **In your notebook, complete the times with the words in the box. Listen, check and repeat.**

half o'clock past quarter ten to

1 It's four ... .
2 It's ... past seven.
3 It's ... past ten.
4 It's quarter ... nine.
5 It's five ... twelve.
6 It's ... to three.

5 **What time is it now?**

6 1.13 **Listen and repeat the Useful language.**

Useful language

Talking about days

What day is it today?
It's Monday/Tuesday, etc.
What day is the Maths lesson?
It's on Wednesday/Thursday, etc.

Talking about times

What time is it?
It's ten o'clock / quarter past nine, etc.
What time is the English lesson?
It's at half past three / quarter to twelve, etc.

Look! **Prepositions of time**

We use *on* to talk about days and *at* to talk about times.
The Science lesson is ***on*** *Monday.*
The Science lesson is ***at*** *nine o'clock.*

7 **Work in pairs. Ask and answer questions about your timetable. Follow the steps in the Speaking plan.**

Speaking plan

Prepare

- Write your timetable for a week.
- Check how to say the school subjects in English.

Speak

- Ask your partner questions from the **Useful language** box to find the days and times of five lessons.
- Use phrases from the **Useful language** box to answer your partner.

Reflect

- How can you improve next time?
- Swap partners and act out a new dialogue.

Now play *Keep moving!*

FAST FINISHER

Choose a day of the week. Write sentences about the time of your lessons.

Maths is at quarter past nine ...

LS Language summary: Unit 1 SB p.118

REAL CULTURE!

Let's learn outside!

I can compare different schools.

A DIFFERENT SCHOOL

The Whole Earth Nature School in the USA is different from most schools. Students aren't in a classroom all day. There aren't computers or laptops. At this school, the lessons are outside in a beautiful forest!

a

LESSONS

The students play a lot of games and the timetable is always interesting. The lessons have animal names.

In 'The Way of the Cougar', students paint their faces and bodies with mud. Now they're the same colour as the forest. They're very quiet, too… shh… Where are they?!

In 'The Way of the Raccoon', students learn about plants. They find edible plants in the forest and make a big salad for lunch. Yum!

In 'The Way of the Owl', students study the animals in the forest. They listen to different birds and look for wild animals and their homes. But they need to be careful – there are black bears here!

In 'The Way of the Wolverine', students make a home in the forest. They make a fire, too!

b

c

TEACHERS

The teachers at Whole Earth are different from your teachers. They have nature names like Lonestar, Thunder and Foxfire. They tell stories and sing songs by the fire. Their clothes are different, too!

d

CLOTHES

There aren't any uniforms at Whole Earth. Students wear T-shirts and they paint them with mud. Their clothes get very dirty!

At this school, the lessons aren't boring. At the end of the school day, the students are tired and dirty, but they are happy!

e

f

1 **Look at the photos of the students at Whole Earth Nature School. Where are the students? What country is the school in?**

2 **1.14 Read and listen to the article and check.**

3 **Match the photos a–f with the blue sentences in the article.**

4 **Read the article again. Complete the sentences with the correct form of *be*.**

1 The Whole Earth school … in the UK.
2 The lessons … in a classroom.
3 The timetable … interesting.
4 'The Way of the Owl' … a lesson about animals.
5 The students … in school uniforms.
6 The students … happy at the end of the school day.

5 **COMPARE CULTURES Work in pairs. Compare your school with the Whole Earth Nature School.**

The lessons in the Whole Earth Nature School are outside. The lessons in my school are in classrooms.

6 **1.15 Read the text. Match the countries in the box with the pictures 1–4. Listen and check.**

Australia	Japan	UK	Uruguay

7 **Word Power Match the words in the box with the clothes in the photos.**

hat	jumper	shirt	shoes	shorts
skirt	socks	tie	trousers	

8 **GET CREATIVE Work in pairs. Design a school uniform.**

9 **Describe your school uniform to the class.**

The hat is pink and green.

Now watch the culture video.

FAST FINISHER

Write a list of good things and bad things about Whole Earth Nature School.

Good things: *no uniforms, …*
Bad things: *no computers, …*

FUN FACT

This is the City Montessori School in Lucknow, India. It is the biggest school in the world. There are more than 50,000 students at the school and there are more than 1,000 classrooms!

SCHOOL UNIFORMS AROUND THE WORLD

In many countries, students wear school uniforms. But the clothes aren't the same in every country. We hear from four students about their school uniform.

1

2

3

4

Me and my school

WRITING A student profile

I can write about myself.

1 **Look at the pictures on the school website. Guess the answers to the questions. Read and check.**

1 Where is the boy from? 2 How old is he? 3 What are his favourite subjects?

Brandon Gate School

Home | Students | Teachers | School Clubs | Latest news | Contact us | Sign in

Gus Winter – Year 8

Hi, my name's Gus and I'm twelve years old. I'm a student at Brandon Gate School and I'm in Year 8. The school is in Bristol, a city in the UK . It's a big school and there are 2,000 students. My favourite day is Wednesday. English and P.E. are my favourite subjects and they're on Wednesday! English is difficult, but it's interesting. P.E. is fun ... football is my favourite sport, but I'm not in the school football team.

2 **Work in pairs. Compare yourselves with Gus.**

Gus is twelve and I'm twelve, too.

I'm not from the UK. I'm from Brazil.

3 **Look at the Useful language. How do you say these expressions in your language?**

Useful language

You and your school

I'm in Year ...
I'm a student at ...
It's a big/small/old/new school.
There are ... students.
My favourite day/subject is ...
I'm (not) in the school ... team.

4 **Read the Look! box. Find examples of capital letters in Gus's profile.**

Look! Capital letters

We use capital letters:

- at the start of sentences: *It's an old school.*
- when we use the subject pronoun *I*: *I'm ten years old.*
- for names of people and places: *My name's Ana and I'm from Madrid.*
- for countries and nationalities: *I'm from Spain and I'm Spanish.*
- for days of the week: *Friday is my favourite day.*

5 **In your notebook, rewrite the sentences with capital letters.**

1 hello, this is edward and he's mexican.
2 today isn't tuesday. it's monday.
3 my name's sonia and i'm from the usa.
4 this is kate. she's eleven years old.
5 it's a small school in birmingham in england.

6 **Write a student profile about you for your school website.**

Writing plan

Prepare

› Make notes about you and your school.
  - Which year are you in?
  - What's the name of your school?
  - Where is it?
  - What's your favourite subject? Why?

Write

› Use your notes to write sentences.
› Use the expressions from the **Useful language** box.

Reflect

› Check your use of capital letters.
› Check your spelling.
› Check your grammar: articles, *be*: affirmative and negative

W **Writing summary** WB p.84 L **Language summary: Unit 1** SB p.118

Friends and family

2

Vocabulary: Family and pets; Countries and nationalities | **Grammar:** Possessives; *be*: questions and short answers | **Speaking:** Introducing yourself | **Writing:** Describing photos

VOCABULARY Family and pets

I can talk about my family and pets.

1 **Copy and complete Josh's family tree with the words in the box.**

aunt brother cat cousin (x2) dad dog fish grandma grandpa mum parrot rabbit sister uncle

2 2.1 **Copy and complete the table with the words from Exercise 1. Listen, check and repeat.**

Male	Female	Male or female	Animals

3 **Draw your family tree with the names of your family and pets.**

4 **Work in pairs. Ask and answer questions about the people in your family tree.**

A: Who is Sarah?
B: Sarah is my mum.
A: Who is Fifi?
B: She's my dog.

Now watch the vlog.

FAST FINISHER

Think about your family. How many people and pets are there? Write a list.

Two uncles, three aunts, a cat ...

Best friends forever

READING

I can scan a text for specific information.

My best friend

A best friend is the number one person in your life. Send us a photo and tell us about your best friend.

1

Hello! I'm Emma and my best friend is Carla. We're both twelve and our birthday is on the 14 November … she's my twin sister! This is a photo of us both. I'm in the red and white T-shirt and Carla is next to me. Her T-shirt is blue.

Hi, my name's Jenny. This is a photo of me with my two BFFs (best friends forever) – Sara and Jack. They're great! We're not in the same class, but we're in the football club together. They're thirteen and I'm only eleven. My big brother is thirteen and he's in their class.

2

3

Hi! I'm Noah and I'm thirteen. My little brother is Ivan and he's six. This is a photo of Ivan's birthday. We're in Bournemouth, a city in the UK. Its beaches are great. Ivan isn't my best friend. My best friend is Max … he's my dog!

4

Hello, my name's Bradley and I'm eleven. I'm an only child (I don't have any brothers or sisters), so my best friend is very important to me. His name is Paul. He's my cousin and he's twelve. His house is near my house and we're always together.

1 2.2 **Read and listen to the text. Match the pictures with the people.**

a Bradley
b Jenny
c Emma
d Noah

2 Scan the text. Copy and complete the table in your notebook.

	Age	Name of best friend(s)
Emma		
Jenny		
Noah		
Bradley		

3 **Word Power** **Find words from the text to complete the sentences.**

1 Emma and Carla are … sisters.
2 Jenny's … brother is thirteen.
3 Noah's … brother is Ivan.
4 Bradley is an … child.

4 Copy the table in your notebook. Ask your classmates the question *Do you have any brothers or sisters?* and complete the table.

Find someone who …	Name:
1 is an only child.	
2 has a big brother.	
3 has a big sister.	
4 has a little brother.	
5 has a little sister.	
6 has a twin sister/brother.	

A: Do you have any brothers or sisters?
B: No, I'm an only child. / Yes, my big brother is sixteen.

FUN FACT

Luis and Jaelyn Valencia are twin brother and sister, but their birthdays are in different years! Jaelyn was born at 11.59 p.m. on 31 December 2015. Luis was born at 12.02 a.m. on 1 January 2016.

GRAMMAR Possessive adjectives

I can use possessive adjectives.

Now watch the grammar animation.

1 Read the grammar box. Choose the correct answers to complete the rules.

Subject pronoun	Possessive adjectives	
I	**my**	I'm David. This is **my** brother.
you	**your**	You're in Class 3. This is **your** classroom.
he	**his**	He's tall. This isn't **his** jacket.
she	**her**	She's happy. Today is **her** birthday.
it	**its**	It's a good dog. This is **its** ball.
we	**our**	We're from the USA. **Our** house is in New York.
they	**their**	They're my friends. **Their** names are Lucy and Tom.

Rules

We use possessive adjectives [1] *before / after* nouns to show that something belongs to someone.

Possessive adjectives are [2] *the same / different* with plural and singular nouns.

2 Complete the sentences with possessive adjectives. Check your answers in the text.

1 I'm Emma and ... best friend is Carla.
2 We're both twelve and ... birthday is on the 14 November.
3 Carla is next to me. ... T-shirt is blue.
4 They're thirteen and I'm only eleven. My big brother is thirteen and he's in ... class.
5 We're in Bournemouth, a city in the UK. ... beaches are great.
6 My best friend is very important to me. ... name is Paul.

Possessive *'s*

I can talk about possession.

3 Copy and complete the grammar box with *'s* or *'*.

Add [1] ... to names and singular nouns.	This is Jack**'s** brother. It's Ivan**'s** birthday.
Add [2] ... to plural nouns that end in *-s*.	My parents**'** car is green.
Add [3] ... to irregular plurals.	That is the women**'s** bathroom.

4 2.3 Read the best friend fact file. Copy and complete the description with the correct answers. Listen and check.

BEST FRIEND FACT FILE	
Boy/Girl:	boy
Name:	Gary
Age:	12
Brothers/Sisters:	Polly (6)
Pet:	rabbit (Snowball)
Same class:	✓
Favourite subject	Art

[1]*His / My* best friend is a boy. [2]*His / Her* name is Gary and he's twelve years old. [3]*Gary' / Gary's* little sister is six years old and [4]*her / our* name is Polly. [5]*Their / Our* pet is a rabbit and [6]*its / your* name is Snowball. Gary is in [7]*my / her* class at school and [8]*his / their* favourite subject is Art.

5 Complete a best friend fact file about your best friend. Write sentences about him/her.

My best friend is a girl. Her name is ...

6 In your notebooks, rewrite the sentences with *'s* or *'*.

Juan best friend is Alicia.
Juan's best friend is Alicia.

1 My cousins house is in the city.
2 The cat toys are blue and green.
3 Your parents car is very fast.
4 The children party is at 3.00.
5 Selina dog is white.

FAST FINISHER

Write six sentences about your classmates' things.

Juan's pencil case is red ...

LS Language summary: Unit 2 SB p.119

Where are they from?

VOCABULARY and LISTENING Countries and nationalities

I can understand information about nationalities.

1 2.4 **Match the countries in the box to the flags. Listen, check and repeat.**

Argentina	Brazil	China	Mexico
Spain	the UK	the USA	Turkey

2 **Copy and complete the sentences with the nationalities in the box.**

American	Argentinian	Brazilian	British
Chinese	Mexican	Spanish	Turkish

WHERE ARE YOU FROM?

I'm from the UK. I'm [1] … .

Rodrygo is [2] … . He's from Brazil.

Selena Gomez is [3] … . She's from the USA.

We're from Turkey. We're [4] … .

Lang Lang is [5] … . He's from China.

Café Tacvba are [6] … . They're from Mexico.

Ricky Rubio is [7] … . He's from Spain.

Mia Maestro is from Argentina. She's [8] … .

3 **PRONUNCIATION Nationalities**

2.5 **Listen and repeat the words.**

American	Argentinian	Brazilian	British
Chinese	Mexican	Spanish	Turkish

4 **Work in pairs. Ask and answer the question from Exercise 2.**

A: Where are you from?

B: I'm from the UK. I'm British.

5 **Work in pairs. Ask and answer questions about other people you know**

A: Where is Lionel Messi from?

B: He's from Argentina. He's Argentinian.

6 2.6 **Read about a radio programme and look at the picture. Guess where Antonio is from. Listen and check.**

International families

PLAY ▶

Some families are from different countries. Today we talk to Antonio Gonzalez. His family is from all over the world.

7 2.6 **Listen again and complete the table with the nationalities.**

Antonio	[1] *Mexican*	grandma	[5] …
mum	[2] …	uncle	[6] …
dad	[3] …	cousins	[7] …
grandpa	[4] …	aunt	[8] …

8 **THINK CRITICALLY** **What are the good things and bad things about having an international family?**

LS Language summary: Unit 2 SB p.119

GRAMMAR *be*: questions and short answers

I can ask *yes/no* questions with the verb *be*.

Now watch the grammar animation.

1 **Read the grammar box. Choose the correct answer to complete the grammar rule.**

Questions	Short answers	
Am I right?	Yes, I **am**.	No, **I'm not**.
Is he/she/it from Mexico?	Yes, he/she/it **is**.	No, he/she/it **isn't**.
Are we/you/they Spanish?	Yes, we/you/they **are**.	No, we/you/they **aren't**.

Rule

In questions the verb *be* comes *before / after* the subject.

2 **In your notebook, put the words in the correct order to make questions from the interview.**

1 from / you / Mexico / are / ?
2 dad / is / American / your / ?
3 dad's / American / are / your / parents / ?
4 Mexican / is / your / aunt / ?

3 2.7 **Match the answers with the questions in Exercise 2. Listen and check.**

a No, they aren't. My grandpa is British and my grandma is Spanish.
b Yes, I am. I'm Mexican.
c No, she isn't. She's Brazilian!
d Yes, he is. He's from Boston.

4 **Work in pairs. Ask questions and give short answers. Try to add more information.**

Are you Spanish?
A: Are you Spanish?
B: Yes, I am. I'm from Madrid.

1 Is the teacher American?
2 Is your notebook yellow?
3 Am I your friend?
4 Are we English students?
5 Is today Monday?

5 2.8 **Look at the table and listen to Dani and Isabella play the 'All about me' game. Why are the words important for Dani?**

All about me:	*Dani*		
Person	**Number**	**Colour**	**Country**
Sandra	*thirteen*	*blue*	*the USA*

6 **Copy and complete the table from Exercise 5 and write important words for you.**

7 **Work in pairs. Play the 'All about me' game. Ask and answer questions about the words.**

8 FIND OUT **Work in pairs. Choose a picture and find out the information.**

1

Name:
Sanna Marin
Age:
Nationality:
Job:

2

Name:
Can Yaman
Age:
Nationality:
Job:

3

Name:
Meghan Markle
Age:
Nationality:
Job:

9 **Read the Look! box. Copy and complete the questions with *is* or *are*.**

Look! **Asking for information**

We often use the verb *be* to ask for information.

What [1] *... his name?*	*His name's Tristan.*
How old [2] *... you?*	*I'm thirteen.*
Where [3] *... they from?*	*They're from the USA.*
What [4] *... her job?*	*She's an actor.*

10 **Work in groups. Ask and answer to find out information about the people in Exercise 8.**

How old is Sanna Marin?

FAST FINISHER

Write questions to interview a classmate.

What's your name? Are you Spanish?

LS Language summary: Unit 2 SB p.119

KEEP TALKING!

Party time!

READING and LISTENING

I can understand an invitation.

1 Look at the invitations. Are they similar or different to party invitations from your friends?

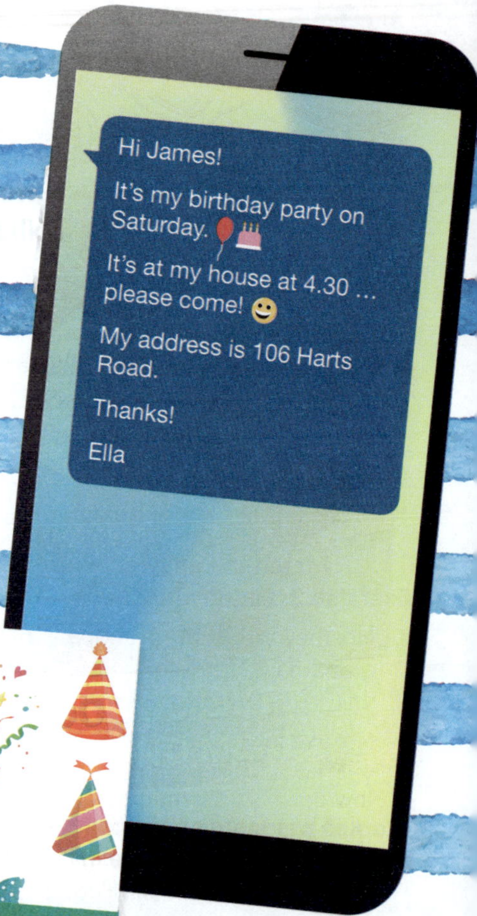

2 **Read the invitations and answer the questions.**

1 What day is Harry's party?
2 What is his mum's phone number?
3 What time is Ella's party?
4 Where is Ella's party?
5 How old is Zoe now?
6 What is her address?

3 **Which party would you like to go to? Why?**

4 2.9 **Listen to James and a friend. Which invitations do they talk about?**

5 2.9 **Listen again and answer the questions.**

1 What is the problem?
2 Why is James happy at the end of the conversation?

SPEAKING Introducing yourself

I can introduce myself and ask questions.

1 2.10 **Listen and read. Where are James and Ava?**

James: Hi, I'm James. What's your name?
Ava: Hello, James. I'm Ava. Nice to meet you.
James: Nice to meet you too, Ava. Where are you from?
Ava: I'm from San Antonio.
James: San Antonio? How do you spell that?
Ava: It's S-A-N A-N-T-O-N-I-O.
James: Is it in Mexico?
Ava: No, it isn't. It's in the USA. I'm American.
James: Oh, OK. How old are you, Ava?
Ava: I'm thirteen. What about you?
James: I'm twelve. It's a good party!
Ava: Yeah, it's great!

2 2.11 **Listen and repeat the Useful language.**

Useful language

Introductions
Hi/Hello.
I'm ... / My name's ...
Nice to meet you (too).

Asking for personal details
What's your name?
Where are you from?
How do you spell that?
How old are you?

3 2.12 **Read the Look! box. Copy the sentences in the correct order in your notebook. Listen and check.**

Look! Asking the same question

We use *What about you?* instead of repeating a question.
A: How old are you?
B: I'm thirteen. ***What about you?***
A: I'm twelve.

a Nice to meet you too, Isabella. How do you spell that?
b I'm from Argentina. What about you?
c I'm fourteen.
d I-S-A-B-E-L-L-A.
e Hi, my name's Yusuf. What's your name?
f Where are you from?
g I'm Isabella. Nice to meet you.
h I'm from Turkey. How old are you, Isabella?

4 Work in pairs. Look at the information in the box. Prepare a new dialogue. Follow the steps in the Speaking plan.

Speaking plan

Prepare
- Imagine you meet for the first time at a party.
- Make notes for your dialogue.

Speak
- Practise your dialogue.
- Use phrases from the **Useful language** box and the *Look!* box.
- Act out your dialogue.

Reflect
- How can you improve next time?
- Choose a new name, age and nationality and swap roles.

5 GET CREATIVE Work in pairs. Design a party invitation for your friends.

Now play *Keep moving!*

FAST FINISHER
Write a dialogue for two famous people meeting for the first time.
A: Hi, I'm Meghan. What's your name?
B: Hi, Meghan. I'm Harry. Nice to meet you.

LS Language summary: Unit 2 SB p.119

REAL CULTURE!

Pets in the UK

I can compare pets in the UK with my country.

PET POWER!

British people love pets. 45% of people in the UK have a pet – that's 20 million animals! But for some people, these animals aren't just pets ... they're part of the family. And these people do EVERYTHING with their pets!

FASHION

Some people buy coats for their pets. The animals stay warm in cold weather. But there are other clothes, too – T-shirts, dresses and even pyjamas! This is a diamond collar for a dog ... it's $150,000!

FOOD AND DRINK

Many cafés in the UK are 'pet-friendly'. This means it's OK for pets to be in the café with their owners. But this is a pet café. The café is full of animals and they even have special menus for the pets.

ENTERTAINMENT

In the UK, there are special TV channels for cats. And this is a 'dog-friendly' cinema! The people are in the cinema with their dogs and they watch a film together! There are blankets and bowls of water for the dogs.

EXERCISE

Many people take their dogs for a walk, but what about this woman? Sarah Smith is from Brighton in the UK, and this is her dog, Louise. Louise is on Sarah's paddle board! But don't worry – it isn't dangerous. Louise has a life-jacket!

1 **Look at the pictures. Which is your favourite?**

2 **2.13 Read and listen to the article about pets. Choose the correct answers.**

1 There are 20 million *people* / *pets* in the UK.
2 The *dog* / *collar* is $150,000.
3 The special menu in the pet café is for *animals* / *people*.
4 The cinema is for *cats* / *dogs*.
5 *Sarah* / *Louise* is the woman.

3 **Word Power** **Match the words in the box with the animals (a–j).**

bird	cat	chicken	dog	fish
hamster	lizard	rabbit	snake	tortoise

TOP TEN UK PETS

4 **2.14 Work in pairs. Which animal is the favourite UK pet? Put the animals in order from 1–10. Listen and check.**

5 **2.15 Work in pairs. Match the celebrities with their pets. Listen and check.**

A: I think that is Leonardo DiCaprio's cat.
B: I don't think it's his pet. I think it's Taylor Swift's cat.

6 **COMPARE CULTURES** **Work in groups. Answer the questions about your country.**

1 Are pets popular in your country?
2 Which animals do people have as pets?
3 What activities can you do with pets?

Now watch the culture video.

FAST FINISHER

Write sentences about your pet or a pet you know.

Lulu is my dog. She's black and white.

Celebrity pets

Can you match these cute pets to their celebrity owners?

My photos

WRITING Describing photos

I can write a post about my photos.

1 **Look at the social media posts. Do you use social media?**

2 **Read Peter's posts and match them to his photos.**

Peter FOLLOW

Hi! My name's Peter. I'm thirteen and I'm from the UK. These are my four favourite photos. They're important people and things in my life.

a This is a photo of my family. It isn't a big family. Those are my parents and that's my little sister. Her name's Olivia and she's eleven years old.

b These are my best friends, Maya and Leo. They're in my English class at school. Maya is British, but Leo isn't from the UK. He's from Spain.

c This is a photo of our pets. Sammy is my dog and Gigi is Olivia's cat. They're different, but they're good friends.

d This is my smartphone. It isn't expensive, but it's important for me – for photos, games and chatting with my friends.

3 **Read the post again. Choose the correct answers.**

1 Peter is *British* / *American*.
2 Olivia is Peter's *big* / *little* sister.
3 Maya and Leo *are* / *aren't* from the same country.
4 Sammy is *Peter's* / *Olivia's* pet.
5 Peter's smartphone *is* / *isn't* cheap.

4 **Read the Useful language. How do you say these expressions in your language?**

Useful language

Describing personal photos

This is a photo of my family / our pet.
These are my parents / my friends.
This is my mother / our house.

5 **Read the Look! box. Find examples of *and* and *but* in Peter's posts.**

Look! *and/but*

We use *and* to add information.
My name is Juan ***and*** *I'm twelve years old.*
We use *but* to contrast information.
My mum is British, ***but*** *my dad is Brazilian.*

6 **Copy and complete the sentences with *and* and *but*.**

1 Hi, my name is Gabriel ... I'm twelve.
2 I'm British, ... my best friend is Spanish.
3 Our car isn't expensive, ... it's fast.
4 I'm with my friends ... I'm happy.
5 My dad is a teacher ... he's at work today.

7 **Write posts about your favourite photos. Follow the steps in the Writing plan.**

Writing plan

Prepare

- Choose four photos of your family, friends, pets or things that are important to you.
- Make notes about the people and things in the photos (age, nationality, other adjectives).

Write

- Use your notes to write sentences.
- Use phrases from the **Useful language** box.
- Connect ideas using *and/but*.

Check

- Check your grammar: possessive adjectives, possessive *'s*, the verb *be*.
- Check *and/but*.
- Check your spelling.

W **Writing summary** **WB** p.85 **L** **Language summary: Unit 2** **SB** p.119

At home

3

Vocabulary: Rooms; Objects in the home | Grammar: *There is / There are*; Prepositions of place | Speaking: Meeting friends | Writing: A chat forum

VOCABULARY Rooms

I can talk about rooms in my home.

Where do you live?

1 3.1 **Match the words in the box with the rooms in Emily and Paulo's homes. Listen, check and repeat.**

balcony bathroom bedroom dining room garage garden hall kitchen living room study

2 3.2 **Listen and match the sounds with the rooms.**

3 Work in pairs. Point at a room in the pictures. Your partner says the name.

That's Paulo's kitchen.

4 Which home is most similar to yours? Which do you prefer? Why?

5 Work in pairs. Imagine your partner comes to your house. Show them your home.

Hi, welcome to my flat. This is the hall ...

6 FIND OUT In the UK, semi-detached houses and terraced houses are typical homes. What is the difference?

Now watch the vlog.

FAST FINISHER

Draw a picture of your home and label the rooms.

LS Language summary: Unit 3 SB p.120

Homes with a difference

READING

I can use pictures to help me understand a text.

Two unusual houses

Are there any unusual houses in your town? Or are they all the same? Today we look at two houses that are VERY unusual!

This is the Keret House in Warsaw, Poland. It's between two other buildings and it's very thin – it's just 122 cm wide! The door is on the street and there are some stairs to the first floor. The kitchen, bathroom and living room are downstairs and there's a bedroom upstairs. The roof is glass and there are two windows, so there's lots of light. The Keret House is popular with writers and artists. So, is there a study? No, there isn't, but there's a desk in the bedroom.

House NA

Keret House

This is House NA in Tokyo, Japan. It's very different to the other houses on the street because there aren't any walls. There are big windows instead. There are three floors and the rooms are on different levels. There's a garage, a living room, a kitchen, a study and there are three bedrooms. There isn't a garden, but there are some big balconies with plants on them. It's modern and beautiful, but the neighbours can see everything you do!

1 **Read the title of the article and look at the pictures. What does *unusual* mean?**

a the same as other things

b different from other things

2 **3.3 Look at the pictures. What's unusual about the two houses? Read, listen and check.**

3 **Word Power Find four parts of houses in the article and match them to the pictures.**

4 **Look at the pictures and read the article again. Copy the table in your notebook and tick (✓) the things the houses have.**

	Keret House	House NA
stairs		
walls		
windows		
a garage		
balconies		
a garden		

5 **THINK CRITICALLY Work in pairs. Say one good thing and one bad thing about the two houses in the article.**

One good thing about the Keret House is ...

GRAMMAR *There is / There are*: affirmative and negative

I can use *there is* and *there are* to talk about rooms.

Now watch the grammar animation.

1 **Read the grammar box. Complete the rules with *a/an*, *any* or *some*.**

	Affirmative	Negative
Singular	**There's (There is) a** bedroom upstairs.	**There isn't a** study.
Plural	**There are some** stairs to the first floor.	**There aren't any** walls.

Rules

We use *there's (there is) / there isn't* + [1] ... + singular noun.

We use *there are* + [2] ... + plural noun.

We use *there aren't* + [3] ... + plural noun.

2 **Look at the table in Exercise 4 on page 30. Copy and complete the sentences with the correct form of *there is / there are* and *a*, *any* or *some*.**

1 ... stairs in the Keret House and in House NA.
2 ... walls in the Keret House, but ... walls in House NA.
3 ... windows in the Keret House and in House NA.
4 ... garage in House NA, but ... garage in the Keret House.
5 ... balconies in House NA, but ... balconies in the Keret House.
6 ... garden in House NA or in the Keret House.

3 **Look at the picture of the house and write sentences with *there is / there are*.**

There's a garden, but there isn't a garage.

There is / There are: questions and short answers

I can use *is there* and *are there* to ask questions.

4 **Read the grammar box. Complete the rules with *a/an* or *any*.**

	Questions	Short answers
Singular	**Is there a** study in the Keret House?	Yes, **there is**. / No, **there isn't**.
Plural	**Are there any** unusual houses in your town?	Yes, **there are**. / No, **there aren't**.

Rules

We use *is there* + [1] ... + singular noun.

We use *are there* + [2] ... + plural noun.

5 **Work in pairs. Ask and answer questions about your home with the words in the box.**

balconies dining room garage garden kitchen stairs study windows

A: Are there any balconies in your house?

B: Yes, there are.

6 **Read the Look! box. Find the answers to the questions in the article on page 30.**

Look! Asking about numbers

We can use *How many ... are there?* to ask about numbers of things.

How many** bedrooms **are there?

There are two bedrooms.

1 How many windows are there in the Keret House?
2 How many bedrooms are there in House NA?
3 How many floors are there in House NA?

7 **Work in pairs. Ask and answer *How many ... are there in the classroom?* with the words in the box.**

bags books boys clocks computers girls phones teachers walls windows

FUN FACT

The 'House in the Clouds' is in Thorpeness, in the UK. There are six floors and the house is 21 metres tall! There's a big living room at the top of the house with fantastic views.

FAST FINISHER

Write sentences about things in your bag.

There are some books in my bag.

LS Language summary: Unit 3 SB p.120

What's in your bedroom?

VOCABULARY and LISTENING Objects in the home

I can listen for the location of objects.

1 **Look at the pictures. Which rooms can you see?**

2 3.4 **Match the words in the box with the objects in the rooms. Listen, check and repeat.**

bed bath cooker fridge light plant
poster shower sofa table toilet wardrobe

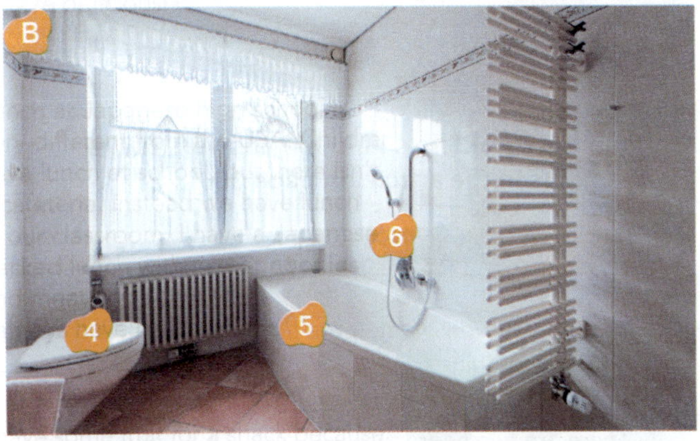

3 **PRONUNCIATION** /ə/ **sound**

3.5 **Listen and repeat the words from Exercise 2.**

1 shower 2 poster 3 sofa 4 cooker

4 **Work in pairs. Take turns to tell your partner about a room in your house. Your partner guesses which room.**

A: There's a table. There isn't a cooker. There's a sofa.

B: Your living room!

5 **Look at the podcast. Is your bedroom similar to Ryan's bedroom or Katie's bedroom?**

6 3.6 **Choose the correct words to complete the sentences. Listen to the podcast and check.**

1 Ryan's bedroom is *tidy / messy*.
2 Katie's bedroom is *tidy / messy*.

7 3.6 **Listen again. Match the objects with the places.**

1	Ryan's shoes	a	behind the door
2	Ryan's books	b	under the bed
3	Ryan's clothes	c	on the shelf
4	Katie's shoes	d	in the wardrobe
5	Katie's books	e	on the floor
6	Katie's clothes	f	in front of the wardrobe

LS Language summary: Unit 3 SB p.120

GRAMMAR Prepositions of place

I can talk about the location of objects.

Now watch the grammar animation.

1 3.7 **Read the grammar box. Match the pictures with the sentences in the grammar box. Listen and check.**

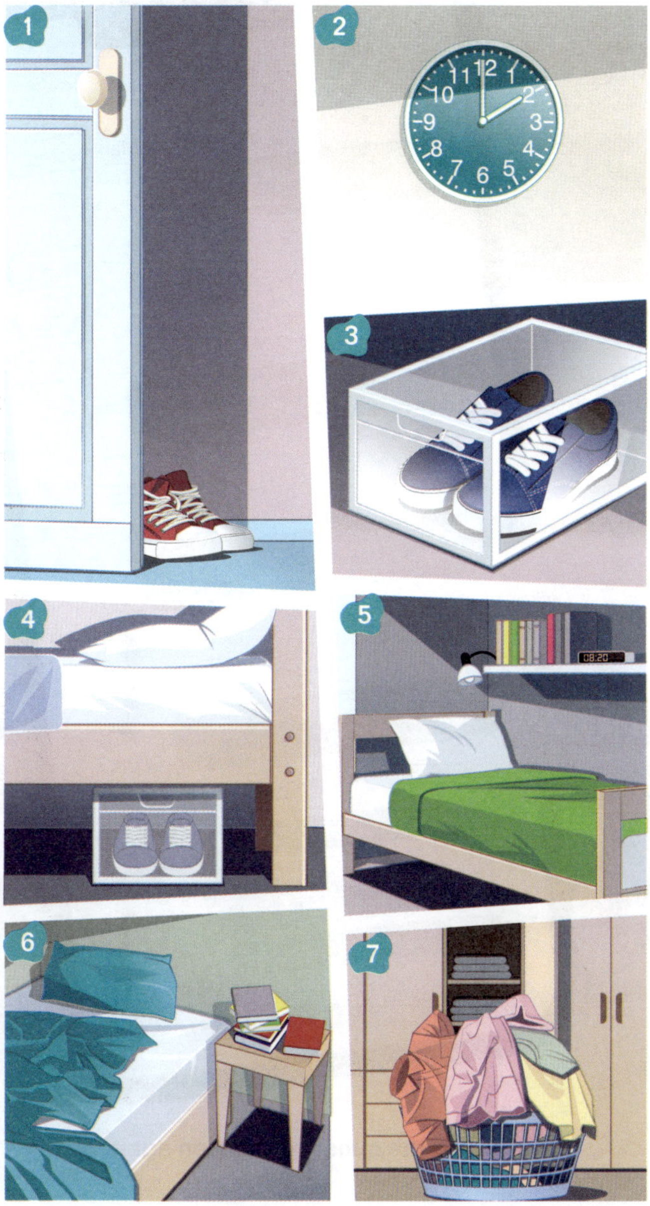

in	The shoes are **in** the box.
on	The clock is **on** the wall.
in front of	The clothes are **in front of** the wardrobe.
next to	The table is **next to** the bed.
behind	The shoes are **behind** the door.
under	The box is **under** the bed.
above	The shelf is **above** the bed.

2 Work in pairs. Make sentences about Ryan's bedroom in Exercise 5 on page 32.

Ryan's shoes are in the box.

3 Look at the picture. Copy and complete the sentences with the correct prepositions of place.

1 There's a chair ... the desk.
2 The poster is ... the plant.
3 There's a ball ... the box.
4 The window is ... the computer.
5 There are some pens ... the desk.
6 The bed is ... the wardrobe.

4 Read the Look! box. Complete the questions with ***Where is*** **or** ***Where are*****.**

Look! Asking about location

We can use *Where is/are ...?* to ask about the location of things.

Where is your book?	*It's on the desk.*
Where are the students?	*They're in the classroom.*

1 ... your bag?
2 ... the clock?
3 ... your notebook?
4 ... your pens?
5 ... your phone?
6 ... the teacher?
7 ... our classmates?
8 ... the window?

5 Work in pairs. Ask the questions from Exercise 4 and answer with prepositions of place.

A: Where is your bag?
B: It's under the desk.

6 GET CREATIVE Work in pairs. Draw a picture of your dream house. Think about rooms and objects. Then present your dream home to the class.

Our house is big. There's a swimming pool on the roof.

FAST FINISHER

Write sentences about a room in your house.

The living room is downstairs. There's a table next to the sofa.

LS Language summary: Unit 3 SB p.120

A new home

READING and LISTENING

I can understand a group chat.

1 **Look at the group chat messages. Whose smartphone is it?**

a Alice b Ruby c Jane

2 **Read the messages about Alice. Choose the correct answer.**

a She's on holiday.
b She lives in a different city now.
c She can't go to school.

3 **Read the messages again. Are the sentences true (T) or false (F)? Correct the false sentences.**

1 Alice is in Manchester.
2 Her new bedroom is small.
3 There are two windows in her bedroom.
4 Alice is happy with pink walls.
5 She is in Ruby and Jane's class at school.
6 Alice's classmates are boring.
7 She wants to see Ruby and Jane.
8 Ruby and Jane are in Manchester on Friday.

4 🔊 3.8 **Listen to the conversation between Alice, Ruby and Jane on Saturday. Why do the girls go upstairs?**

5 🔊 3.8 **Answer the questions. Listen again and check.**

1 Where are the boxes?
2 Where is Alice's dad?
3 Where is her little brother?
4 Where is her mum?
5 Where are the snacks?

SPEAKING Meeting friends

I can greet friends when I meet them.

1 3.9 **Look at the picture. Guess the relationship between Alfie and Sara. Listen, read and check.**

a brother and sister b classmates c friends

Alfie: Hi, Sara! How are you?
Sara: Good afternoon, Alfie. I'm fine, thanks. How are things?
Alfie: Not bad, thanks.
Sara: How's school?
Alfie: It's OK. Some lessons are difficult ... but that's normal, right?
Sara: Yeah. Hey, there's a new café in the town centre. Do you want to go?
Alfie: Sorry, I'm late for football club.
Sara: Oh, OK. See you later.
Alfie: Bye, Sara. See you on Saturday.
Sara: Saturday?
Alfie: Jake's birthday party is on Saturday.
Sara: Of course ... goodbye!

2 3.10 **Listen and repeat the Useful language. How do you say the expressions in your language?**

Useful language

Greetings
Hi! / Hello!
Good morning/afternoon.
How are you? / How are things?
(I'm) fine / (I'm) good / Not bad, thanks.
Bye. / Goodbye. / Goodnight.
See you later/tomorrow/on Saturday.

3 3.11 **Copy and complete the dialogue with the words in the box. Listen and check.**

bad fine good goodbye how see things

Student: [1]... morning, Mr Robinson.
Teacher: Hello, James. How are [2]...?
Student: Not [3]..., thanks.
Teacher: [4]... are you?
Student: I'm [5]..., thanks. Sorry I'm late.
Teacher: Late? You aren't late!
Student: But the Science class is at 10.00.
Teacher: Yes, the Science class is at 10.00 – tomorrow!
Student: Oh no! [6]... you tomorrow, Mr Robinson.
Teacher: [7]..., James.

4 **Work in pairs. Prepare a new dialogue. Follow the steps in the Speaking plan.**

Speaking plan

Prepare
- Choose the relationship between you (friends, classmates, etc.)
- Decide where you meet each other.
- Make notes for your dialogue.

Speak
- Practise your dialogue.
- Use phrases from the **Useful language** box.
- Act out your dialogue without notes.

Reflect
- How can you improve next time?
- Swap partners and prepare a new dialogue.

Now play *Keep moving!*

FAST FINISHER

Write a dialogue between two friends on a chat group like the one on page 34.

A: *Hi, Rosa! How are things?*
B: *I'm fine. How are you?*

LS Language summary: Unit 3 SB p.120

REAL CULTURE!

Modern families

I can compare family homes in the UK with my country.

ALL UNDER ONE ROOF!

Who lives in your home? Is it just you, your parents and your brothers and sisters … or are there others? Two types of family are now common in the UK – the multigenerational family and the blended family.

THE BLENDED FAMILY: THE GIBSON-STONE FAMILY

My name's Zach. My mum is married to Alan – he's my stepdad. Alan has two children, Sophie and Leo. They're my stepbrother and stepsister. My mum is their stepmum. Leo is eleven, I'm twelve and Sophie is fourteen. We do lots of things together. I share a bedroom with Leo – it's usually very messy! And Sophie helps me with my homework! I'm happy because they're my new brother and sister. In August, we all go on holiday together!

MY NAME'S ZACH AND THIS IS MY HOM
I LIVE WITH FOUR OTHER PEOPLE.

THE MULTIGENERATIONAL FAMILY: THE NORTON FAMILY

My name's Izzy and I'm thirteen. I live on the first floor of our house with my mum and dad. My grandparents live downstairs in a flat on the ground floor. My big sister Amy lives upstairs – she's 23 and she's a teacher. There's a small bathroom next to her bedroom. She shares our kitchen – the house is very busy in the morning! We all have lunch together on Sunday, and on Fridays we have a cinema night in our living room. Sometimes I go downstairs and watch TV with my grandma and grandad – it's quiet in their flat!

MY NAME'S IZZY AND THIS IS MY HOME.
I LIVE HERE WITH FIVE OTHER PEOPLE.

1 **Look at the pictures on page 36. Guess who Zach and Izzy live with.**

I think Zach lives with ... *I think Izzy lives with ...*

2 **3.12 Read and listen to the article. Match the people with the names in the box.**

Alan	Amy	Izzy	Izzy's grandparents
Izzy's parents	Leo	Sophie	Zach	Zach's mum

3 **Read the article again. Complete the sentences with a name in the box.**

Amy	Izzy	Leo	Sophie
The Gibson-Stone family	The Norton family		

1 ... helps Zach with his homework.
2 ... have a cinema night.
3 ... shares a kitchen with Izzy and her parents.
4 ... watches TV with grandparents.
5 ... shares a bedroom with Zach.
6 ... go on holiday together.

4 **Word Power** **Find family words in the article for the definitions.**

1 Your mum's husband, but not your father.
2 Your dad's wife, but not your mother.
3 The son of your mum or dad's partner, but not your brother.
4 The daughter of your mum or dad's partner, but not your sister.

5 **COMPARE CULTURES** **In pairs, answer the questions.**

1 Do children and grandparents live in the same home in your country?
2 Are stepbrothers and stepsisters common in your country?

6 **Work in pairs. Do the quiz about two famous homes.**

Buckingham Palace

1 It's in *London / Oxford* in the UK.
2 It's *Prince William's / the Queen's* home.
3 There are *175 / 775* rooms.
4 There are *78 / 148* bathrooms.
5 There's a *football pitch / swimming pool*.
6 *50 million / 15 million* tourists visit it every year.
7 It's worth more than *£2 million / £2 billion*.

The White House

1 It's in *New York / Washington DC* in the USA.
2 It's *the president's / Mark Zuckerberg's* home.
3 There are *32 / 132* rooms.
4 There are *35 / 48* bathrooms.
5 There's a *bowling alley / baseball field*.
6 There are *6,000 / 60,000* visitors every day.
7 It would cost *$397 million / $3.9 billion* to buy.

7 **3.13 Listen and check your answers. Which home would you like to visit?**

Now watch the culture video.

FAST FINISHER

Write sentences about the people in your home.

My two little brothers are in the same bedroom. Their bedroom is very messy.

My home, your home

WRITING A chat forum

I can write a post for a chat forum.

1 **Look at the pictures. Guess where Sinéad is from. Read the chat forum post and check.**

TEEN CHAT

HOME ABOUT CHAT MEMBERS CONTACT

Sinéad O'Connel
Posted: *10 September*

Hi, everyone!

This is a photo of my house. It's in Dublin, Ireland. In our house, there are three bedrooms, a living room and a kitchen. There are two bathrooms. One is downstairs and one is upstairs. My bedroom is next to my parents' bedroom. There's a small garden in front of the house and a big garden behind the house. That's our car in front of the garage. It isn't in the garage because the garage is full of boxes and old furniture - there isn't any space for the car!

Please tell me about your home. Where is it? Is it the same as my house or is it different?

Thanks!

REPLY LIKE SHARE •••

2 **Read the chat forum post again. Copy and complete the table in your notebook. Add a tick (✓), a cross (✗) or the correct number.**

1 living room	
2 study	
3 garden	
4 bedroom	
5 bathroom	
6 garage	

3 **Look at the Useful language. How do you say the expressions in your language?**

Useful language

Describing family homes

My house/flat is in ...
In our house, there are ...
Our flat is on the first/second/third floor.
My bedroom is next to / above / in front of ...
In front of / behind / next to the house, there's a ...

4 **Read the Look! box. Find an example of each type of punctuation in Sinéad's post.**

Look! Punctuation

We use a full stop (.) at the end of a sentence:
My bedroom is next to my parents' bedroom.
We use a comma (,) to separate items in a list:
There are three bedrooms, a living room and a kitchen.
We use a question mark (?) at the end of a question:
Where's your bedroom?
We use an exclamation mark (!) to show emotion:
Your garden is beautiful!

5 **Write a reply to Sinéad about your home. Follow the steps in the Writing plan.**

Writing plan

Prepare

- Make notes about your house.
  - Is it a house or flat?
  - Which rooms are there?
  - Is there a garden/garage/balcony?

Write

- Write your chat forum post.
- Use the expressions from the **Useful language** box.
- Use the punctuation marks from the *Look!* box.

Reflect

- Check your grammar: *There is* / *There are* and prepositions of place.
- Check your punctuation is correct.
- Check your spelling.

W **Writing summary:** WB p.86
R **Review: Units 1–3** SB pp.100–101
P **Project: Units 1–3** SB pp.106–107
L **Literature: Units 1–3** SB pp.112–113
LS **Language summary: Unit 3** SB p.120

Food and drink

4

Vocabulary: Food and drink; Meals | **Grammar:** *like / don't like; would like* | **Speaking:** Ordering in a café | **Writing:** A blog post

VOCABULARY Food and drink

I can talk about food and drink.

1 4.1 **Match the words in the box with the pictures. Listen, check and repeat.**

apple banana butter cake carrot cheese chicken chocolate coffee eggs fish ice cream juice meat milk orange potato tea tomato water

2 Work in pairs. Point at a picture. Your partner says the food or drink.

A: What's that?
B: It's chocolate

A: What are they?
B: They're eggs.

3 Copy the table in your notebook. Complete it with the words from Exercise 1. Some words can go in more than one group.

Fruit and vegetables	Food from animals
apple	*milk*
Sweet food	**Drinks**
chocolate	*juice*

4 Work in pairs. Can you add two words to each group?

5 Work in pairs. Say what's in the fridge and cupboards in your kitchen.

In my fridge, there's some milk and some eggs, but there isn't any juice.

Now watch the vlog.

FAST FINISHER

Write a list of food and drink you like ☺ and food and drink you don't like ☹

☺ *chocolate …*

☹ *coffee …*

LS Language summary: Unit 4 SB p.121

Do you like chocolate?

READING

I can transfer information from a text into a table.

1 4.2 **Read and listen to the article. Choose the correct answer.**

a The people talk about popular food in their country.
b The people talk about their favourite food and drink.
c The people talk about their family's favourite food.

YOUNG SUPER-CHEF

Young Super-chef **is a new TV show. Children aged 10–13 from around the world are in a competition to cook delicious food.**

Today we speak to Marcia, Ethan and Zeynep – three children from the show. We ask them questions about the food they like ... and the food they don't like!

Hi, I'm Marcia. I'm eleven and I'm Brazilian.

DO YOU LIKE MEAT?

No, I don't! I don't like meat or fish because I'm vegetarian. It isn't easy because there's a lot of meat in Brazil! I like fruit and vegetables – they're healthy. My favourite vegetables are carrots and tomatoes. I like sweet food, too. Today is my birthday – and birthday cake is my favourite cake! Mmmm!

My name's Ethan. I'm twelve years old and I'm from the USA.

DO YOU LIKE FISH?

No, I don't. I don't like fish. Urgh – it's horrible! I like meat and I like fruit and vegetables, too. My favourite fruit is bananas and I have a big glass of orange juice in the morning. I don't like chocolate or ice cream – they're sweet and they're very unhealthy!

Hello, I'm Zeynep. I'm thirteen and I'm from Turkey.

DO YOU LIKE FISH AND MEAT?

Yes, I do. I like meat and fish. I like vegetables, too, but I don't like fruit. My favourite food is *menemen*. It's eggs, tomatoes, cheese and vegetables. And I like sweet food. My favourite is ice cream – it isn't healthy, but it's delicious!

2 **Read the article again. Copy the table in your notebook. Complete it with ticks (✓) and crosses (✗).**

	Marcia	Ethan	Zeynep
meat	✗		
fish			
fruit			
vegetables			
sweet food			

3 **Word Power** **Find five adjectives to describe food in the article. How do you say them in your language?**

delicious ...

4 **THINK CRITICALLY** **Work in pairs. Write two lists of healthy and unhealthy food and drink. Compare with another pair. Do you have the same food and drink in your lists?**

GRAMMAR *like / don't like*

I can talk about the food I *like* and *don't like*.

Now watch the grammar animation.

1 **Read the grammar box. Complete the rules with *do* or *don't*.**

Affirmative	Negative
I **like** fish.	I **don't like** meat.
I **like** eggs.	I **don't like** biscuits.
Questions	**Short answers**
Do you **like** chocolate?	Yes, I **do**. / No, I **don't**.

Rules

We use [1] ... with negative sentences.

We use [2] ... with questions.

2 **Look at the table from Exercise 2 on page 40. Copy and complete the sentences in your notebook. Check your answers in the article.**

I [1] ... meat, but I [2] ... fruit and vegetables.

I [3] ... fish, and I [4] ... chocolate or ice cream.

I [5] ... meat and fish, but I [6] ... fruit.

3 **Write sentences for you about the food and drink in the box.**

bananas cake coffee fish ice cream meat milk tomatoes

I like bananas.

4 **Work in pairs. Compare your sentences.**

I like bananas, but you don't like bananas.

5 **PRONUNCIATION** **Linking**

4.3 **Listen and repeat the questions.**

1 Do you like meat?
2 Do you like fish?

6 **Work in pairs. Ask your partner the questions. Reply so the answer is true for you.**

1 Do you like meat?
2 Do you like fish?
3 Do you like vegetables?
4 Do you like fruit?
5 Do you like sweet food?

7 **Work in pairs. Ask your partner about the food and drink. Use short answers and try and give extra information.**

1

2

3

4

5

6

7

8

A: Do you like apples?
B: Yes, I do. They're healthy!
A: Do you like cheese.
B: No, I don't. It's horrible.

FAST FINISHER

Write sentences about the food you like and don't like from your country.

I like burritos. They're delicious!

Lunchtime!

VOCABULARY and LISTENING
Meals

I can identify the meals people want.

1 4.4 **Look at the school menu. Match the meals in the box with the times (A–D). Listen, check and repeat.**

breakfast	dinner	lunch	snacks

2 4.5 **Match the words in the box with the pictures (1–16). Listen and check.**

biscuits	bread	burger	cereal	chips
crisps	nuts	omelette	pancakes	pasta
pizza	rice	salad	sandwich	soup	toast

3 Work in pairs. Ask and answer *Do you like ...?* with the food from Exercise 2.

A: Do you like biscuits?

B: Yes, I do! They're delicious!
No, I don't. They're unhealthy.

4 4.6 **Listen to two students in the cafeteria. Which meal do they have?**

a breakfast
b lunch
c dinner
d a snack

5 4.6 **Listen again. In your notebook, write what Max and Kim have.**

1 **Kim:** ... and ...
2 **Max:** ... and ...

6 Read the Look! box. Write the food and drink you have for your meals. Compare with a partner.

Look! ***have* + meals**

We say: *I have ... for breakfast/lunch/dinner/a snack.*
*e.g. I **have** cereal **for breakfast**.*

I have chicken and rice for lunch.

LS **Language summary: Unit 4** **SB** p.121

GRAMMAR *would like*

I can use *would like* to ask for and offer things.

Now watch the grammar animation.

1 Read the grammar box. Choose the correct answer to complete the rules.

Affirmative	
I'd like (I **would like**)	a burger / some ice cream (please).
Questions	
Would you **like**	a drink? / some chips?
Answers	
Yes, please. / No, thanks.	

Rules

We use *I'd like ..., please* to [1] *ask for / offer* things.

We use *Would you like...?* to [2] *ask for / offer* things.

2 4.7 **Copy and complete Max and Kim's dialogue. Listen and check. Practise the dialogue with a partner.**

Kim: I'd [1] ... some soup, please.
Server: Would [2] ... like a drink?
Kim: [3] ... , please. I'd like some water.
Max: [4] ... like an omelette, please.
Server: No problem. [5] ... you like some bread?
Max: Yes, [6] ... .
Server: OK ... and would you [7] ... some water?
Max: No, [8] ... .

3 Work in pairs. Imagine you are at Highbury College. Choose a meal time and have a conversation.

A: Hi! Would you like breakfast?
B: Yes, please. I'd like ...

like and *would like*

I can understand the difference between *like* and *would like*.

4 Read the grammar box. Copy and complete the rules with *like* and *would like*.

like / don't like	***would like***
I **like** ice cream. It's delicious! I **don't like** carrots. They're horrible.	I'**d like** a burger. I'm hungry. I'**d like** some water. I'm thirsty.
Do you **like** coffee? Yes, I **do**. / No, I **don't**.	**Would** you **like** some milk? **Yes, please.** / **No, thanks.**

Rules

We use [1] ... to talk about things we like or don't like in general.

We use [2] ... to ask for things and offer things.

5 4.8 **Copy and complete the dialogues with the correct answers. Listen and check.**

1 **A:** [1] *I like / I'd like* some soup, please.
B: [2] *Do you like / Would you like* tomato soup or chicken soup?
A: [3] *I like / I'd like* some tomato soup, please. [4] *I don't like / I wouldn't like* chicken.

2 **A:** [5] *Do you like / Would you like* a cheese and tomato omelette?
B: [6] *I like / I'd like* cheese, but [7] *I don't like / I wouldn't like* tomatoes.
A: OK. [8] *Do you like / Would you like* a cheese omelette?
B: Yes, please!

6 Work in pairs. Ask and answer questions about the food using *Do you like ...?* or *Would you like ...?*

A: Would you like some banana pancakes?
B: No, thanks. I like pancakes and I like bananas, but I'm not hungry.

7 FIND OUT *World Food Day* happens on the same day every year. Find out the date of *World Food Day*. What do people do on this day?

FUN FACT

Rita Ora is a British singer and actor. She has the same thing for breakfast EVERY DAY. She always has fish and eggs!

FAST FINISHER

Imagine your dream meals for one day. Write sentences and ask for them.

For breakfast, I'd like some pancakes and orange juice.
For lunch, I'd like ...

LS Language summary: Unit 4 SB p.121

KEEP TALKING!

What's on the menu?

READING and LISTENING

I can understand a menu.

Daisy's Beach Café

Lunch Menu

Sandwiches and snacks

Chicken sandwich	£3.25
Egg salad sandwich	£2.95
Soup of the day	£2.75
Chips	£1.95

Desserts

Ice cream	£1.50
Chocolate biscuits	£1.75
Chocolate and banana cake	£2.50

Mains

Cheese and tomato pizza	£6.95
Chicken and rice	£8.50
Burger and chips	£7.50
Vegetable pasta	£6.95

Drinks

Orange juice	£1.50
Water	£1.00
Coffee	£2.50
Tea	£2.20

1 **Work in pairs. Discuss the questions.**

1 What is your favourite restaurant or café?
2 What type of food is there?
3 What do you usually have there?

2 **Read the menu. In your notebook, write down the names and prices of the food and drink.**

1

2

3

4

3 **Read the Look! box. How do you say the prices of the food in Exercise 2? What is the total price?**

Look! **Prices**

£1.50 = one pound fifty
$2.99 = two dollars ninety-nine
€8.20 = eight euros twenty

4 **Work in pairs. Ask and answer the questions** *How much is the ...?* **with food and drink on the menu.**

A: *How much is the ice cream?*
B: *It's £1.50.*

5 4.9 **Look at the menu and listen to Ivy and Olly. What food and drinks do they want?**

6 4.9 **Listen again. Are the sentences true (T) or false (F)? Correct the false sentences.**

1 The food is expensive.
2 The menu is on the wall.
3 Olly likes pasta and pizza.
4 Ivy likes tomatoes.
5 Olly has three desserts.

SPEAKING Ordering in a café

I can order food and drink in a café.

1 4.10 **Read and listen to Ivy and Olly order their meals. How much does the food cost?**

Server:	Hello, how can I help you?
Ivy:	Hi, I'd like a chicken sandwich and some ice cream, please.
Server:	OK … and anything to drink?
Ivy:	Can I have an orange juice, please?
Server:	Sure.
Ivy:	How much is that?
Server:	That's £6.25 altogether. And what would you like?
Olly:	I'd like a burger, some ice cream and some water, please. Does the burger come with chips?
Server:	Yes, it comes with chips. Anything else?
Olly:	That's all, thanks.
Server:	OK, that's £10.00.
Olly:	Thank you.

2 4.11 **Listen and repeat the Useful language.**

Useful language

Ordering in a café

Server

How can I help you?
What would you like?
Anything to drink? / Anything else?
It comes with …
That's … altogether.

Customer

I'd like …, please.
Can I have …, please?
Does … come with …?
That's all, thanks.
How much is that?

3 4.12 **In your notebook, write the sentences in the correct order. Listen and check.**

a **Server:** Hello. What would you like?
b **Server:** That's £2.75, please.
c **Server:** Yes, it comes with bread. Anything else?
d **Server:** Anything to drink?
e **Customer:** That's all, thanks. How much is that?
f **Customer:** Thanks.
g **Customer:** Hi, I'd like some soup, please.
h **Customer:** No, thanks. Does the soup come with bread?

4 Work in pairs. Use the menu on page 44 to order food and drinks. Follow the steps in the Speaking plan.

Speaking plan

Prepare

› Decide who is the customer and who is the server.
› Choose your food and drink.

Speak

› Practise your dialogue.
› Use phrases from the **Useful language** box.
› Act out your dialogue without notes.

Reflect

› How can you improve next time?
› Swap roles and act out a new dialogue.

5 GET CREATIVE Work in pairs. Design a menu for a new restaurant.

- Think of a name for your restaurant.
- Think of the food and drink at your restaurant. Is it traditional food from your country?
- Decide on the prices of the meals. Are they cheap or expensive?
- Design your menu and present it to the class.

Now play *Keep moving!*

FAST FINISHER

Write a dialogue between a customer and a server. Use your menus from Exercise 5.

Server: Hello, how can I help you?

LS Language summary: Unit 4 SB p.121

A family meal

I can compare British meals with meals in my country.

A Sunday roast?

a

In many countries, friends and families have a special meal at the weekend. In the UK, this time is usually Sunday lunch and the traditional meal is a 'Sunday roast'. This is meat – like chicken – cooked in the oven with potatoes and vegetables. It comes with a sauce called gravy. But these days, many young people don't want traditional British food every Sunday, so today we ask British teenagers what their favourite Sunday lunch is.

1 Holly
Brighton, UK

On Sundays, my family often has a nut roast for lunch. It's full of nuts, mushrooms, carrots and onions and it's cooked in the oven. There isn't any meat in our Sunday roast because my brother is vegetarian – he doesn't eat meat or fish. I'm not vegetarian, but I like vegetarian food!

b

2 Romesh
Birmingham, UK

Sunday lunch is a very important meal for my family. Everyone comes to our house – my aunts and uncles, my cousins and my grandparents! My favourite meal is curry. It's Indian food with chicken or lamb in a delicious sauce with peppers. We have it with rice and bread.

c

3 Sammy
Oxford, UK

On Sundays, our family goes to my grandparent's house. My grandad's speciality is lasagne. It's layers of pasta, with a meat sauce of beef, tomatoes and carrots … and cheese on top – it's delicious! There's a big salad of lettuce and tomato, too. We all eat and talk for hours.

d

1 **Look at the pictures of the meals (a–d) in the text. Match them with the names in the box.**

curry lasagne nut roast Sunday roast

2 4.13 **Work in pairs. Guess which food is in the meals? Read and listen to the text and check your answers.**

In the Sunday roast, there's chicken …

3 **Read the text again and choose the correct answers.**

1 In the UK, people have a special family meal on *Saturday / Sunday*.
2 Many young people want *the same / different* food every week.
4 Holly *is / isn't* vegetarian.
5 On Sunday, Romesh's *family / friends* have lunch at his house.
6 Sammy's *grandmother / grandfather* cooks lunch on Sunday.

4 **Word Power** **Look at the six food words in blue in the text. Copy the table in your notebook and put the words in the correct columns.**

Meat	Vegetables

5 **Read the Famous Food Quiz. Match the meals with the pictures.**

6 4.14 **Work in pairs. Do the quiz. Listen and check your answers.**

7 **COMPARE CULTURES** **Work in pairs. Ask and answer the questions.**

1 When do you have a big meal with your family?
2 How many people are there? Who are they?
3 What food do you have at these meals?
4 What is your favourite family meal?

FUN FACT

Bubble and Squeak is a traditional British dish. You use potatoes and vegetables from the Sunday roast. Fry the potatoes and vegetables together in a pan and as they cook, they make some funny sounds – bubble and squeak!

Now watch the culture video.

FAST FINISHER

Write sentences about your favourite meal.

My favourite meal is enchiladas. It's …

FAMOUS Food Quiz

1

People eat millions of burgers every day. The beef and onions with tomato sauce is delicious. Where are the first hamburgers from?

a The USA
b The UK
c Germany

2

The word 'sandwich' comes from the Earl of Sandwich, a rich British man in the 18th century. He wanted a quick meal of meat and vegetables between two pieces of bread because …

a he only had one arm.
b it's easy to play cards and eat at the same time.
c it's easy to eat outside.

3

The classic Italian pizza with tomato, cheese and basil is sometimes called a Pizza Margherita. Who or what is Margherita?

a Queen Margherita of Italy
b A chef called Margherita Esposito
c It's the name for the Italian flag

4

Caesar Salad with lettuce, cheese and eggs is popular all over the world. Who made the first Caesar Salad?

a Julius Caesar (Emperor, Rome, 60 BC)
b Caesar Cardini (Chef, Tijuana, Mexico, 1924)
c Frank Sinatra (Singer, Caesars Palace Hotel, Las Vegas, 1962)

My weekly food blog

WRITING A blog post

I can write a blog about what I eat.

1 **Look at the pictures in Tammy's blog. Where is she from? Where is she now? Read the blog and check.**

Home • About • Blog • Contact

Posted: 8 May

A week of Japanese food

Hi, my name's Tammy. I'm thirteen and I'm from the USA. I'm in Tokyo for one year. This blog is about my life in Japan. This is what I eat in a typical week.

Breakfast

Many Japanese people have rice and fish for breakfast. I like fish … but not for breakfast! I have a typical American breakfast. I have cereal and milk, or toast and butter. At the weekend I have pancakes – they're delicious!

Lunch

Lunch at Japanese high school is very different from the USA. Children have lunch at school, but there isn't a cafeteria. Instead we have lunch in our classroom. I have a Japanese packed lunch with rice or noodles and meat and some fruit.
I always have milk to drink.

Snacks

I have some fruit for a snack because I don't like Japanese snacks. There are some strange flavours … like green tea and chocolate!

Dinner

I have Japanese meals like meat or fish with vegetables for dinner. But I sometimes have American dinners too, like hamburgers or meatloaf, and Friday is pizza night – my favourite pizza is barbecue chicken.

2 **Read the blog again. Copy and complete the table. Tick (✓) the things Tammy eats.**

Meal	Japanese	American	Both
Breakfast			
Lunch			
Snack			
Dinner			

3 **Look at the Useful language. How do you say these expressions in your language?**

Useful language

Describing your diet

This is what I eat In a typical week.
Many people have ..., but I have ...
There is/isn't a school cafeteria.
I have a packed lunch / school dinners.
My favourite ... is ...
It's delicious/horrible/healthy/unhealthy/sweet.

4 **Read the Look! box. Choose the correct words to complete the sentences.**

Look! ***and/or***

We use *and* to say we have two things together.
We use *or* to say we have one of two options.
*I have cereal **and** milk.* = cereal + milk
*I have cereal **or** toast.* = cereal / toast

1 I drink milk *and* / *or* orange juice in the morning.
2 I have bread *and* / *or* butter for breakfast.
3 I would like a burger *and* / *or* some chips, please.
4 For dessert, there are biscuits *and* / *or* ice cream.
5 She likes rice *and* / *or* noodles for lunch.

5 **Write a blog about what you eat in a typical week. Follow the steps in the Writing plan.**

Writing plan

Prepare

› Make notes about the food you eat for breakfast, lunch, dinner and snacks. Think about:
- the food I like for breakfast, lunch etc.
- the food I don't like
- where I eat it
- what is different at weekends

Write

› Write your blog post with an introduction and a heading for each meal.
› Use the expressions from the **Useful language** box.
› use *and/or* to talk about what you eat.

Check

› Check your grammar: *like / don't like*.
› Check you use *and/or* correctly.
› Check your spelling.

My life

Vocabulary: Daily routine; Common verbs | Grammar: Present simple: affirmative and negative | Speaking: Making and responding to suggestions | Writing: An article

VOCABULARY Daily routine

I can describe my daily routine.

1 5.1 **Match the daily routines with the pictures. Listen, check and repeat.**

do (my) homework   finish school   get dressed   get home   get up   go to bed   have a shower
have breakfast (lunch/dinner)   leave home   make a snack   start school   study Maths (English, etc.)

2 5.2 **Complete the text with the correct verbs. Listen and check.**

My day
by Anna

Hi, my name's Anna and this is my typical day. I [1]... up at 7.15, then I [2]... a shower and [3]... dressed. At 8.00, I [4]... breakfast and then I [5]... home. I [6]... school at 9.00 and we [7]... Maths and English in the morning. I [8]... lunch at 1.00 and we [9]... Science in the afternoon. I [10]... school at 3.30 and I [11]... home at 4.00, then I [12]... a snack because I'm hungry. I [13]... my homework in the evening and [14]... dinner at 7.30. I [15]... to bed at 10.30 at night.

3 **Read the Look! box. Which activities does Anna do at the different times of day?**

Look! Times of the day

in the morning (05.00–12.00)   *in the evening* (17.00–21.00)
in the afternoon (12.00–17.00)   *at night* (21.00–05.00)

In the morning, Anna gets up, has a shower ...

4 **Work in pairs. Describe your typical day.**

I get up at 7.00 in the morning ...

Now watch the vlog.

FAST FINISHER

Write sentences about your routine at the weekend.

On Saturday, I get up at 10.00 in the morning ...

LS Language summary: Unit 5 SB p.122

An actor's life for me!

READING I can interpret information.

SAME FAMILY, DIFFERENT DAYS

My name's Charlotte and I'm twelve years old. This is Jordan – he's my twin brother. We're the same age, but our days are very different. I go to a typical school near our house, but Jordan goes to a theatre school in London.

It's a special school for actors, dancers and musicians. He studies English, Maths and Science, but he also studies Dance, Singing and Drama! His school is interesting, but his days aren't easy. He gets up early – 5.30 in the morning – because his school is far from our house. He leaves home at 6.30 and he starts school at 9.00. My dad drives Jordan and he has breakfast in the car!

I start school at 9.00, too, but I get up at 7.45 and I have breakfast at home. I finish school at 4.00 and I do my homework in the afternoon. Jordan finishes school at 6.00 and he does his homework … in the car! He gets home late, but we have dinner together.

Jordan's days are long and difficult, but he's happy. He wants to be a famous actor! I'm happy, too – I like my school and I have good friends … and I get up late!

1 5.3 **Read and listen to the article about Charlotte and Jordan. Are they happy at their schools?**

2 Read the article again. Are the sentences true for Charlotte (C), Jordan (J) or both (B)?

1 I'm twelve years old.
2 My school is in London.
3 I get up at quarter to eight.
4 I start school at nine o'clock.
5 I do my homework in the car.
6 I have dinner with my family.

3 Which school day do you like most: Charlotte's or Jordan's?

I like Charlotte's day because …

4 Word Power Match the blue words with the pictures.

1 

2 

3 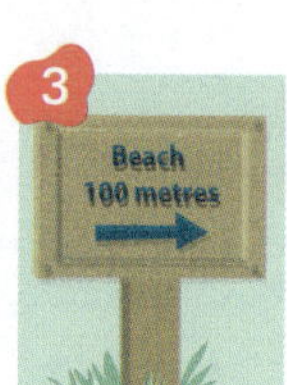

4 

5 Work in pairs. Ask and answer the questions.

1 Is there a café near your house?
2 Is your school far from your house?
3 Are you early for school?
4 Are you late for school?

6 FIND OUT The Brit School is a theatre school in the UK for young actors, musicians and artists. Which of these famous people wasn't a student at the Brit School?

Adele, singer

Tom Hiddleston, actor

Jessie J, singer

Tom Holland, actor

GRAMMAR Present simple: affirmative

I can use the present simple.

Now watch the grammar animation.

1 **Read the grammar box and complete the rules with *-s*, *-ies*, and *-es*.**

I/We/You/They	**get up** at 7.45 in the morning. **go** to a typical school. **study** English, Maths and Science. **have** breakfast at home.
He/She	**gets** home late. **goes** to a theatre school. **studies** Dance and Drama. **has** breakfast in the car.

Rules

When the subject is *he*, *she* or *it*, we usually add [1] ... to the verb.

For verbs ending in *-ch*, *-sh*, *-ss*, *-x* and *-o* we add [2] ... to the verb.

For verbs ending in *-y*, we omit *-y* and add [3] ... .

For the verb *have*, we use *has*.

2 **Copy and complete the sentences with the correct form of the verbs in brackets. Check your answers in the article on page 50.**

1 I ... to a typical school near our house. (go)
2 Jordan ... to a theatre school in London. (go)
3 He ... English, Maths and Science. (study)
4 Jordan ... home at 6.30. (leave)
5 He ... breakfast in the car. (have)
6 I ... school at 4.00. (finish)
7 Jordan ... his homework in the car. (do)
8 We ... dinner together. (have)

3 **PRONUNCIATION Third person *-s***

5.4 **Listen and repeat.**

/s/	/z/	/ɪz/
gets	leaves	finishes

4 5.5 **Copy and complete the table in Exercise 3 with the words in the box. Listen, check and repeat.**

drives goes likes starts
teaches watches

5 5.6 **Work in pairs. Guess which options are correct for the daily routines of the people. Listen and check.**

I think Adekemi gets up at 6.00 in the morning. Then she has coffee and toast for breakfast ...

1

Adekemi Okunbo: Footballer

2

Dani Russo: DJ

3

Joao Sousa: Writer

get up?	8.00 in the evening	6.00 in the morning	10.00 in the morning
breakfast?	eggs, fish, fruit	coffee, toast	cereal, fruit juice
start work?	12.00 at night	3.00 in the afternoon	8.00 in the morning
finish work?	5.00 in the morning	10.00 at night	2.00 in the afternoon
go to bed?	10.00 at night	2.00 in the afternoon	12.00 at night

6 **Copy and complete the sentences with information about yourself.**

1 I get up at ... and I have ... for breakfast.
2 I start school at ... .
3 I study ... .
4 I have ... for dinner.
5 I go to bed at ... .

7 **Compare your sentences in pairs. Make sentences about you and your partner.**

I get up at 7.00, but Silvia gets up at 7.30.
We have cereal for breakfast.

FUN FACT The American actor Mark Wahlberg has a very unusual daily routine. He gets up at 2.30 in the morning, has breakfast at 3.15, goes to the gym and then has a shower for an hour and a half!

FAST FINISHER

Imagine a famous person's daily routine and write sentences.

Justin Bieber gets up at ...

LS Language summary: Unit 5 SB p.122

Home school

VOCABULARY and LISTENING Common verbs

I can understand information in a podcast.

1 5.7 **Copy and complete the phrases with the verbs in the box. Listen, check and repeat.**

call drink eat know live meet
teach travel use want wear work

1

... in a flat

2

... your parents

3

... your friends

4

... water

5

... a laptop

6

... a uniform

7

... a new phone

8

... the answer

9

... in an office

10

... pizza

11

... English

12

... by bus

2 Copy and complete the sentences with verbs from Exercise 1. Tick (✓) the sentences that are true for you.

1 I ... my friends in the park.
2 I ... in Spain.
3 I ... my grandparents every week.
4 I ... jeans and a T-shirt at the weekend.
5 I ... the names of all my classmates.
6 I ... orange juice.
7 I ... a pet rabbit for my next birthday.
8 I ... a dictionary in my English class.
9 I ... to school by bike.
10 I ... meat.

3 Compare your sentences in pairs. Tell the class about your partner.

Alex meets his friends in the park.

4 5.8 **Look at the picture and read about the podcast. Can you guess why Josh doesn't go to school? Listen and check.**

I don't go to school

Josh's day starts like most twelve year olds. He gets up in the morning and gets dressed. Then he has breakfast ... but he doesn't go to school. Listen to the podcast and find out why.

Listen Download

5 5.8 **Listen again. Are the sentences true (T) or false (F)?**

1 Josh's mum teaches him.
2 A Spanish teacher goes to his house.
3 He uses computers in his classes.
4 He meets his friends every day.
5 He has exams at the end of the year.
6 He wears a uniform.

6 **THINK CRITICALLY** **Work in pairs. Make a list of good and bad things about homeschooling. Is it a good idea in your opinion?**

LS Language summary: Unit 5 SB p.122

GRAMMAR Present simple: negative

I can use present simple negative.

Now watch the grammar animation.

1 Read the grammar box. Complete the rules with *don't* or *doesn't*.

I/You/We/They	**don't** (**do not**)	**go** to school.
He/She	**doesn't** (**does not**)	**wear** a uniform.

Rules

When the subject is *I*, *you*, *we* or *they* we use [1] ... + infinitive.

When the subject is *he*, *she* or *it* we use [2] ... + infinitive.

e.g. *Josh doesn't go to school.* NOT ~~*Josh doesn't goes to school.*~~

2 Rewrite the sentences in the negative form using *don't* or *doesn't*. Which sentences are true for you?

1 I have toast for breakfast.
2 My best friend lives near me.
3 I travel to school by bus.
4 My phone has a camera.
5 My parents work at home.
6 My teacher wears a T-shirt.

3 Complete the text with the affirmative (+) or negative (–) form of the verbs in brackets.

Alma Deutscher is British, but she [1] ... (– live) in the UK. She [2] ... (+ live) in Vienna, Austria. She's famous because she plays the violin and the piano and she writes music, too. She only writes happy music because she [3] ... (– like) sad music. Alma [4] ... (– go) to school because her parents [5] ... (+ teach) her at home. They [6] ... (– teach) her music because she's too good. All of Alma's friends are on social media, but she [7] ... (– use) it. In fact, she [8] ... (– have) a smartphone!

Present simple: questions and short answers

I can ask and answer questions in the present simple.

4 Read the grammar box. Choose the correct answers to complete the rules.

Questions			Short answers
Do	I/you/we/they	**go** to school?	Yes, I/you/we/they **do**. No, I/you/we/they **don't**.
Does	he/she	**wear** a uniform?	Yes, he/she **does**. No, he/she **doesn't**.

Rules

In present simple questions, *do* and *does* go [1] *after / before* the subject.

When the subject is *he*, *she* or *it*, we [2] *add / don't add -s* to the infinitive.

5 Look at Exercise 5 on page 52. Work in pairs. Ask and answer questions about Josh.

Josh's mum / teach him

Does Josh's mum teach him?

Yes, she does.

1 a Spanish teacher / go to his house
2 he / use computers in his classes
3 he / meet his friends every day
4 he / have exams at the end of the year
5 he / wear a uniform

6 Work in pairs. Ask and answer questions. Use the ideas in Exercise 5.

A: Does your mum teach you?

B: No, she doesn't.

7 Work in small groups. Ask and answer questions about the activities below. Give more information with your answers.

do homework in the morning
eat fish
know the people on your street
live with your grandparents
meet friends in the evening
want a new phone
wear shorts at the weekend

FAST FINISHER

Write questions and answers for an interview with a classmate.

A: *Do you meet your friends after school?*
B: *No, I don't.*

LS Language summary: Unit 5 SB p.122

KEEP TALKING!

After-school fun

READING and LISTENING

I can understand information on notice boards.

1 **Read about four different clubs. Which of the clubs are at school?**

After-school Clubs & Activities

Meet and eat

Do you like food from different countries? We're a group of students from Year 8 and we love food and drink! On Friday afternoons, we meet and make food from around the world. We try Chinese food, Brazilian food … even British food! Come to classroom C3 at 3.30 p.m. next Friday – it's free!

MOVIE LOVERS

Do you like films? We go to the Phoenix cinema on Wednesday evenings and we watch new films. Cinema tickets are cheap (£5) because we buy group tickets. After the film, we go to *Harry's Café*. We have a snack and a drink and we talk about the film. Text Julia on 07700 900317 today and join our club!

Study group

We're a study group and we want new people. We meet in classroom B12 at 4.00 p.m. on Tuesdays and Thursdays. We study and do our homework for two hours. We also ask questions when the work is difficult. It's easy when you're with other people! Call Daniel on 20180563 and see you soon!

Stage Stars

Saturday 10.00–1.00 at The Littlefield Theatre

Professional singers and dancers teach children aged 10–15. Students have one hour of singing, one hour of dance and one hour of drama. Email Katherine at katdance@stagestars.org for prices and more information.

2 **Read the notices again. Which club(s) …**

1 doesn't cost any money?
2 is at the weekend?
3 has food and drink?
4 is a class with teachers?
5 is at two different places?
6 is on two different days?

3 **Which club would you like to try? Are there after-school clubs like this at your school?**

4 5.9 **Listen to a dialogue between Ruby and George. Which clubs do they talk about?**

5 5.9 **Listen again and answer the questions.**

1 Does George go to football practice at the weekend?
2 Does Ruby have some difficult Science homework?
3 Does George do his homework in the afternoon?
4 Does Ruby like Brazilian food?
5 Is George hungry in the afternoon?

SPEAKING Suggestions

I can make and respond to suggestions.

1 5.10 **Listen and read. What do Ruby and George decide to do?**

Ruby: Hi, George. How are you?
George: Oh, hi, Ruby. I'm fine, thanks. I don't have homework tonight!
Ruby: Me neither. Would you like to do something together?
George: That's a good idea.
Ruby: Do you want to go to the shopping centre?
George: I think it's too far.
Ruby: Come on! You want a new T-shirt.
George: Sorry, but I don't feel like it.
Ruby: OK. What about that movie club? It's Wednesday today.
George: Maybe. What film is it tonight?
Ruby: The new *Spiderman* film.
George: That sounds great! Let's text Julia and join the club.

2 5.11 **Listen and repeat the Useful language.**

Useful language

Suggesting	Responding
Would you like to ...?	That's a good/great idea!
Do you want to ...?	That sounds good/great!
What about ...?	I think it's too expensive/cold/late.
Let's ...	Sorry, but I don't feel like it.
Why don't we ...?	Maybe.

3 5.12 **Copy and complete the dialogue with the words in the box. Listen and check.**

good like maybe that think want what why

Freya: Hi, Max. How are things?
Max: Not bad, thanks. How are you?
Freya: Good, thanks. Do you [1] ... to meet after school tomorrow?
Max: That's a [2] ... idea. [3] ... don't we go to the beach?
Freya: I [4] ... it's too cold for the beach. Would you [5] ... to go to the cinema?
Max: [6] ... . Or [7] ... about the park near my house? There's a new basketball court.
Freya: [8] ... sounds great! See you tomorrow.

4 **Work in pairs. Make and respond to suggestions about the clubs on page 54. Follow the Speaking plan.**

Speaking plan

Prepare
- Choose three clubs to use in your dialogue.
- Think of one good thing and one bad thing about each club.

Speak
- Greet each other and suggest joining a club.
- Use phrases from the **Useful language** box.
- Agree on a club to go to together.

Reflect
- How can you improve next time?
- Swap roles and act out a new dialogue.

Now play *Keep moving!*

FAST FINISHER

Think of a club and write a notice.

Come to Science club. It's on Tuesday afternoon ...

LS Language summary: Unit 5 SB p.122

REAL CULTURE!

Away from home

I can compare summer activities in the USA with my country.

SUMMER CAMPS IN THE USA

What do you do in the summer holidays? In the USA, 14 million young people go to summer camps. They stay there for 2–8 weeks and they make new friends, learn new things and have fun! Let's hear from Madison. She's at Camp Riverside in New Hampshire for the first time.

1 ...

There are a hundred children at camp right now. All the girls' cabins are together in one place and all the boys' cabins are in a different part of the camp. There are ten girls in my cabin. My bed is next to Alicia's bed – she's my new best friend!

2 ...

We get up at 8.00 and have a shower. After breakfast we choose a team sport. There's football, tennis and basketball, but my favourite is softball because I'm good at it!

3 ...

Yes, we eat together in the dining hall. After lunch, everyone is tired and we have a 'rest hour'. Some people sleep, but I talk with Alicia or hang out with friends and play cards or something like that.

4 ...

The afternoons because it's time for adventure sports! Everyone gets very excited because we try new activities, like horse riding, mountain biking or archery. My favourite is white-water rafting. I was scared at first, but now I love it!

5 ...

I was sad in the beginning because I missed my family, but now I'm very happy because I have a lot of new friends. At home I use social media a lot and call my friends every day. I don't do that here because smartphones aren't allowed. It isn't easy, but I'm never bored because there are a lot of fun activities.

6 ...

No, we don't. In the evenings, we sit by a fire and sing songs. It's great!

1 5.13 **Look at the pictures and read the introduction. What do you think Madison likes and doesn't like about summer camp? Read and listen to the text and check.**

2 **Read the text again. Match the questions with paragraphs 1–6.**

a How many people are there at Camp Riverside?
b Do you go to bed early?
c What's the most difficult thing about summer camp?
d What do you do in the morning?
e What's your favourite part of the day at summer camp?
f Do you have lunch with your friends?

3 **Word Power** **Look at the blue adjectives in the text. Choose the best answers to make the sentences true for you.**

1 I feel tired ...
in the morning / at night / at school.
2 I feel happy ...
at school / at home / outside.
3 I feel bored ...
at the cinema / in English class / in Maths class.
4 I feel excited ...
before a party / when I watch sport / when I play games.
5 I feel sad ...
on Sunday evenings / when I'm alone / when I watch sad films.

4 **COMPARE CULTURES** **Work in pairs. Discuss the questions.**

1 What do young people do in the summer holidays in your country?
2 Are there any summer camps?
3 Are they similar to the summer camp in the text?
4 When do young people spend time away from their families?

5 **Look at the map of Camp Riverside. Match the words in the box with the parts of the map.**

archery	boys' cabins	dining hall	football
girls' cabins	health centre	horse riding	
mountain biking	shower block	softball	
tennis	white-water rafting		

6 5.14 **Listen. Where are the people? Choose from the places on the map.**

7 **GET CREATIVE** **Work in pairs. Draw a map of a summer camp with all the activities you would like to try.**

Now watch the culture video.

FAST FINISHER

Write three or four sentences about you and Madison and the things you like and don't like.

Madison's favourite sport is softball, but my favourite sport is football.

Madison likes white-water rafting, but I don't like it.

My typical day

WRITING An article

I can write about a typical day in my country.

1 Read the introduction to the article. Work in pairs. Guess the answers to the questions.

1 Do British teenagers wear a school uniform?
2 What do British teenagers have for breakfast?
3 How do British teenagers go to school?
4 What time does school start in the UK?
5 What do British teenagers have for lunch?
6 What time does school finish in the UK?
7 What do British teenagers do in the evening?
8 What time do British teenagers go to bed?

2 Read the article and check your answers for Exercise 1.

A DAY IN THE LIFE OF A TEENAGER

Every week a reader describes a typical day for teenagers in their country. This week it's Isla from the UK.

ISLA, 13, UK

Most British teenagers wear a school uniform, so the first thing they do is get up and get dressed. Usually, they don't have a big breakfast – maybe just cereal or toast. Then they leave home. Some teenagers walk to school, but others go in the car or travel by bus because they live far from the school.

In the UK, most schools start at about 9.00 and finish at about 3.30. There's an hour break for lunch. Usually, there are hot meals in the cafeteria, but some students eat food from home – like sandwiches and fruit. When school finishes, some students go home, but others stay at school because they go to after-school clubs.

Most families have dinner at about 6.00. After dinner, British teenagers watch TV, play games, do homework or use their phones to call friends or go on social media. Usually, they go to bed at about 10.00 at night. But at the weekend, they go to bed late and get up late because there isn't school!

3 Read the Useful language box. How do you say these expressions in your language?

Useful language

Describing general habits

In the UK, most people/schools ...
Some students/schools ..., but others ...
Usually, ...
... at about 9.00/10.00.

4 Read the Look! box. Find examples of *because* in the article.

Look! ***because***

We use *because* to explain the reason for something.
We leave home early ***because*** *our house is far from school.*
I get up late ***because*** *I don't like mornings!*

5 Match sentences 1–6 with sentences a–f. Join the sentences with *because* and write them in your notebook.

1 We don't have dinner with our mum.	a School starts at 9.00.
2 I don't like Maths.	b There's a Drama club after school.
3 I get home late on Tuesday.	c I'm hungry.
4 I go to bed early.	d It's boring.
5 We leave home at 8.30.	e I'm very tired.
6 I make a snack in the afternoon.	f She works in the evening.

6 Write an article about a teenager's typical day in your country. Follow the steps in the Writing plan.

Writing plan

Prepare

- Think about a typical day in your country. How is it different to a day in the UK?
- Answer the questions in Exercise 1 about teenagers in your country.

Write

- Write your article.
- Use the expressions from the **Useful language** box.
- Use *because* to give reasons.

Reflect

- Check your grammar: present simple.
- Check your punctuation is correct.
- Check your spelling.

W Writing summary WB p.88 **L Language summary: Unit 5 SB** p.122

Free time

Vocabulary: Free-time activities; Dates and seasons | **Grammar:** Adverbs and expressions of frequency; *Wh-* questions | **Speaking:** Asking for information | **Writing:** An email

6

VOCABULARY Free-time activities

I can talk about my free time.

1 6.1 **Complete the phrases with the verbs in the box. Use each verb twice. Listen, check and repeat.**

go   listen to   play   read   visit   watch

1 

2 

3 

4 

5 

6 

7 

8 

9 

10 

11 

12 

2 Copy and complete the questions with verbs from Exercise 1.

1 Do you ... the piano?
2 Do you ... TV with your family?
3 Do you ... books in bed?
4 Do you ... shopping with your friends?
5 Do you ... music in your bedroom?
6 Do you ... on holiday to different countries?
7 Do you ... videogames with your friends?
8 Do you ... interesting podcasts?
9 Do you ... museums with your family?
10 Do you ... online videos on your phone?

3 Work in pairs. Ask and answer the questions from Exercise 2.

4 Work in pairs. Can you think of more free-time activities with the verbs from Exercise 1.

go to the park, listen to the radio ...

5 Work in pairs. Which free-time activities do you do at the times in the box?

in the morning   in the afternoon
in the evening   at the weekend

In the morning, I listen to music.

Now watch the vlog.

FAST FINISHER

Write sentences about your partner's free time.

At the weekend, Nuria visits her family.

LS **Language summary: Unit 6 SB** p.123

I check YouTube fifty times a day!

READING

I can read for detail.

1 **Work in pairs. Ask and answer the questions.**

1 Which videogames do you play?
2 Do you know any professional gamers?
3 What type of videos do you watch on YouTube?
4 Who is your favourite YouTube star?

2 6.2 **Look at the pictures. Why are Lewis and Ellie famous? Read and listen to the webpage and check.**

Home Articles Contact

Free-time fun for internet stars

There are two very popular free-time activities for teenagers: they watch online videos and they play videogames. But what about teenage YouTube stars and professional gamers? What do *they* do in their free time?

Lewis Huang, professional gamer

I play videogames every day because I'm an esports player. I get up early and practise in the morning, then my fans watch me play in competitions in the evening. Millions of people stream my games, so it's important that I play well.

In my free time, I go to the park or the beach because I never go outside in my job! I also go to the gym twice a week. I'm always in my chair at work, so it's important to do exercise. People think my life is easy, but it isn't! I'm always very tired in the evening. I download a film every week and watch it with my friends, but I usually fall asleep!

More

Ellie White, YouTube star

I play the guitar and I use the YouTube website for my music. I upload a new video once a week and I have fans in lots of countries! People post comments under my videos. They sometimes write bad comments like, 'I don't like this song!' but most people are nice about my music.

I don't have much free time because I go to school and I make music. In the evening, I usually listen to music and I read books. I never watch TV because it's boring. Before I go to bed, I read the comments about my songs. I check YouTube fifty times a day!

3 **Read the webpage again. Are the sentences true (T) or false (F)?**

1 Lewis watches other people play videogames.
2 Lewis goes to the gym in the evening.
3 Lewis thinks his life is difficult.
4 People in different countries watch Ellie's music videos.
5 Ellie watches TV in the evening.
6 Ellie doesn't read the comments about her music videos.

4 **Word Power** **Look at the blue words in the webpage. Ask and answer the questions with a partner.**

1 What are your favourite websites?
2 Do you stream music or do you download it?
3 Do you upload photos to social media websites?
4 Do you post comments about photos and videos?

5 **THINK CRITICALLY** **Imagine there is no internet. How does your life change? Think about the ideas in the box.**

free time friends and family school and homework shopping

I don't chat with friends on social media. We meet and talk together.

GRAMMAR Adverbs of frequency

I can use adverbs of frequency to say how often I do things.

Now watch the grammar animation.

1 **Read the grammar box. Choose the correct answers to complete the rules.**

100%	I'm **always** very tired in the evening.
	I **usually** fall asleep.
	They **sometimes** write bad comments.
0%	I **never** watch TV.

Rules

Adverbs of frequency come [1] *before / after* the verb *be*.

Adverbs of frequency come [2] *before / after* other verbs.

2 **Rewrite the sentences with the adverbs of frequency in the correct places.**

1 I play videogames before school. (never)
2 I'm bored in my English lessons. (sometimes)
3 I visit friends or family at the weekend. (usually)
4 My bedroom is very tidy. (usually)
5 I travel to school by bus. (always)
6 My parents listen to music in the kitchen. (sometimes)
7 My teacher is late for class. (never)
8 I'm happy in the mornings. (always)

3 **Change the adverbs of frequency in Exercise 2 so the sentences are true for you. Compare with a partner.**

Expressions of frequency

I can use expressions of frequency to talk about how often I do things.

4 **Read the grammar box. Complete the rules with the correct words.**

I play videogames **every day**.
I download a film **every week**.
I upload a new video **once a week**.
I also go to the gym **twice a week**.
I check YouTube **fifty times a day**!

Rules

We say [1] ... *day/week/year*.

We say *once*, [2] ..., *three times a day/week/year*.

Expressions of frequency come at the [3] ... of the sentence.

5 **Order the expressions of frequency in the box from 1 (most frequent) to 7 (least frequent).**

every day every month every week four times a week once a year ~~twice a day~~ twice a month

1 twice a day ...

6 6.3 **Match the phrases with the best expressions of frequency. Listen and check.**

1 I brush my teeth ... a every summer.
2 I have a shower ... b twice a day.
3 I go to the dentist ... c once a month.
4 I go to the cinema ... d five times a day.
5 I drink water ... e every day.
6 I go on holiday ... f twice a year.

I brush my teeth twice a day.

7 **Work in pairs. Are the sentences in Exercise 6 true for you? If not, make them true.**

8 **Read the Look! box. Work in pairs. Ask and answer *How often do you ...?* for the activities in the box.**

Look! ***How often ...?***

We use *How often ...?* to ask questions about frequency.
***How often** do you go to the cinema?*
*I go to the cinema **once a month**.*

do homework go shopping listen to music play videogames read books visit your cousins visit museums watch a film

A: How often do you do homework?
B: I do homework every day.

FUN FACT

Andy Park is from Wiltshire in the UK. People call Andy 'Mr Christmas' because it's always Christmas at his house. He celebrates Christmas 365 times a year!

FAST FINISHER

Write sentences about how often you and your family do things.

I meet my friends every weekend.
My brother never watches TV.

LS Language summary: Unit 6 SB p.123

Festival time

VOCABULARY and LISTENING Months, dates and seasons

I can listen for specific details.

1 6.4 **Match the seasons with the pictures. Listen, check and repeat. Which is your favourite season?**

autumn spring summer winter

2 6.5 **Put the months in the correct order. Listen, check and repeat.**

April August December February
January July June March May
November October September

3 Match the months with the season for your country.

Winter is December, January and February.

4 6.6 **Match the numbers with the dates. Listen, check and repeat.**

1st	eighth	11th	fourteenth
2nd	tenth	12th	thirty-first
3rd	first	13th	twentieth
4th	seventh	14th	fifteenth
5th	second	15th	thirtieth
6th	ninth	20th	twenty-second
7th	sixth	21st	eleventh
8th	fifth	22nd	twelfth
9th	third	30th	thirteenth
10th	fourth	31st	twenty-first

5 6.7 **Write the dates in words. Listen and check.**

1 Christmas Day: the ... of ... (25/12)
2 Halloween: the ... of ... (31/10)
3 American Independence Day: the ... of ... (4/7)
4 Valentine's Day: the ... of ... (14/2)

6 Look at the pictures of four different festivals. Which countries and seasons do you think they show?

Las Fallas

Harbin Ice and Snow Festival

Holi

Songkran

7 6.8 **Listen to a radio programme. Which festival does Lian talk about? Why does she like it?**

8 6.8 **Listen again. Copy and complete the fact file about the festival.**

Name of festival: *Harbin Ice and Snow Festival*
Country: [1] ...
Month/Date: [3] ...
Season: [2] ...
Number of visitors: [4] ...
What?: *Ice sculptures*

9 FIND OUT Look for information about the Holi, Las Fallas and Songkran festivals. Complete fact files for these festivals.

10 Which festival from this lesson would you like to go to? Why?

LS Language summary: Unit 6 SB p.123

GRAMMAR *Wh-* questions

I can ask *Wh-* questions.

Now watch the grammar animation.

1 **Read the grammar box. Copy and complete the rules with the correct question words.**

Question word	*do/does*	Subject	Infinitive
What	do	people	wear at the festival?
When	does	it	start?
Where	does	Lian	live?
Why	does	she	like the festival?
Who	does	she	go with?

Rules

We use [1] ... to ask about people.
We use [2] ... to ask about things.
We use [3] ... to ask about places.
We use [4] ... to ask about times.
We use [5] ... to ask about reasons.

2 6.9 **Match answers a–e with the questions in the grammar box. Listen and check.**

a On 5th January.
b In Beijing in China.
c Because it's beautiful and exciting.
d Her grandparents.
e They wear big coats and hats.

3 **PRONUNCIATION Question words**

6.10 **Listen to the question words in the box. Is *Wh-* pronounced the same way in all the words? Listen again, check and repeat.**

What When Where Who Why

4 6.11 **Read the next part of the programme. Complete the presenter's questions with the correct question words. Listen and check.**

Presenter: [1] ... do you live, Alex?
Alex: I live in Valencia, in Spain. I want to talk about *Las Fallas*. It's a festival in my city.
Presenter: [2] ... do people do at *Las Fallas*?
Alex: They make big puppets and then they set fire to them!
Presenter: They set fire to them? Wow! [3] ... do you like the festival, Alex?
Alex: Because the city is very busy and noisy!
Presenter: It sounds fun! [4] ... do you go with?
Alex: I go with my friends.
Presenter: [5] ... does the festival start?
Alex: On 15th March.

5 **Put the words in the correct order to make questions. Write the answers in your notebook.**

1 where / go at the weekend / you / do / ?
2 do / who / call every day / you / ?
3 meet your friends / do / you / when / ?
4 you / what / watch on TV / do / ?
5 why / like your favourite singer / do / you / ?

6 **Work in pairs. Ask and answer the questions from Exercise 5.**

A: Where do you go at the weekend?
B: I usually go to a shopping centre.

7 **Choose a topic from the box. Write *Wh-* questions about this topic.**

holidays free time a festival weekends

Where do you go on holiday?
Who do you go with?
What do you do there?
Why do you like it?

8 **Work in pairs. Ask and answer your questions from Exercise 7.**

A: Where do you go on holiday?
B: I go to the south of Spain.
A: Who do you go with?
B: I always go with ...

FAST FINISHER

Imagine there is a new student in your class. Write questions to find out about his/her life.

Where do you live?

KEEP TALKING!

How much are the tickets?

READING and LISTENING

I can understand a poster for an event.

1 **Look at the poster for a festival called Tweenfest. What activities does it have? Which activity would you like to try most?**

THE LANSBURY TWEENFEST

SATURDAY 15TH APRIL

A ONE-DAY FESTIVAL FOR 11–13 YEAR OLDS

Make a pizza

Learn to make a pizza and cover it with your favourite toppings. Drink a free lemonade while we cook your pizza!

Zorbing

Do you like adventure sports? Are you twelve or older? Come and try zorbing – it's fun, fast and safe.

Fancy-dress competition

The theme this year is… ANIMALS! We want to see you as dogs, cats, birds … and there's a £20 prize for the best costume!

Ukulele class

Our teacher, Sam Carter, teaches you three easy tunes in just one hour! And he sells ukuleles at the end of the class.

Paintballing

Do you want to try paintballing? We have a game for beginners in Lansbury Park. This activity is very popular – call Gavin now on 04432 872319 to buy a ticket.

For more information, visit our website www.lansburytweenfest.com or call our team on 0117 496235.

2 **Read the poster again. Answer the questions.**

1 When is the festival?
2 How much does the lemonade cost?
3 What is the minimum age for zorbing?
4 What does the person with the best fancy dress win?
5 Who is the teacher for the ukulele class?
6 Where is the paintballing game?

3 **6.12** **Listen to Jessica and Callum talk about the festival. Which activity do they want to try?**

4 **6.12** **Listen again and answer the questions.**

1 Does Callum know about Tweenfest?
2 What does he think about zorbing?
3 What musical instrument does Callum play?
4 Who does he visit on Saturday?
5 What time does he leave home?
6 What does Callum do to find out more information about the festival?

SPEAKING Asking for information

I can ask for and give information.

1 6.13 **Callum calls the organizers of Tweenfest. Listen and read. Does the person answer all of Callum's questions?**

Organizer: Hello, this is Tweenfest.
Callum: Oh, hi. I'd like to ask some questions about the festival.
Organizer: Yes. What would you like to know?
Callum: First, what time does it start?
Organizer: It starts at 10.00 in the morning.
Callum: And how much are the tickets?
Organizer: Tickets are £10.
Callum: OK, and what time is the ukulele class?
Organizer: The ukulele class starts at 11.30 and finishes at 12.30.
Callum: Great. And one more thing. How much do the ukuleles cost?
Organizer: I'm sorry, but I don't have that information.
Callum: So, who can I contact about that?
Organizer: You need to speak to Sam Carter. His email address is on our website.
Callum: OK. Thanks very much.

2 6.14 **Listen and repeat the Useful language.**

Useful language

Asking for information
What time does it start/finish?
How much are the tickets?
How much do/does ... cost?
Who can I contact about ...?
Is there a ...? / Are there any ...?

Giving information
It starts at ... / It finishes at ...
Tickets are ...
Sorry, but I don't have that information.
You need to speak to/contact/email ...

3 6.15 **Put the dialogue in the correct order. Listen and check.**

1 g

a It starts at 7.30.
b Great. How much does it cost to park for three hours?
c Yes, there is. It's next to the theatre.
d Hi. What time does the show start tonight?
e That's OK. Thanks for your help.
f Tickets are £10.00 or £20.00.
g Hello, this is the Beckett Theatre. How can I help you?
h That's cheap. Is there a car park near the theatre?
i OK ... and how much are the tickets?
j Sorry, but I don't have that information.

4 **GET CREATIVE** **Work in pairs. Design a poster for a festival. Choose a name and include important information and fun events.**

5 **Work in pairs. Find out information about a festival. Follow the steps in the Speaking plan.**

Speaking plan

Prepare
- Decide on your roles.
- Use your poster from Exercise 4 or the poster on page 64.
- Make notes for your dialogue.

Speak
- Practise your dialogue.
- Use phrases from the **Useful language** box.
- Act out your dialogue without notes.

Reflect
- How can you improve next time?
- Swap roles and act out a new dialogue.

Now play *Keep moving!*

FAST FINISHER
Think of an event in your country that you would like to go to. Write questions and answers about it.
A: *How much are the tickets?*
B: *Tickets are 50 Euros.*

LS Language summary: Unit 6 SB p. 123

REAL CULTURE!

UK music festivals

I can compare music festivals in the UK with events in my country.

Festival Fun

Music festivals are very popular in the UK. Every summer, there are more than 500 outdoor festivals and millions of people go to them. And it's not just adults – many younger people go with their parents. Here are three of the best.

Glastonbury Festival

Freddie, 12

When? Five days in June

Big or small? Very big! 200,000 people, 2,000 bands

How much? Aged 13 and over: £248; aged 12 and under: free

I go to Glastonbury with my family every summer. I love it because there's every type of music here from rock and dance music to jazz and classical. We always see some very famous bands. But there are some things I don't like. It's very noisy at night, and it's too big – it's like a busy city! And when it rains, it's awful!

Deer Shed Festival

Maya, 11

When? Three days in July

Big or small? Small: 10,000 people, 60 bands

How much? Aged 11–15: £70; adult: £100

Deer Shed is my favourite festival. My family comes every year and we always meet my friends and their parents. It's a small, safe festival, so I can hang out with my friends and then meet my parents later. And it's not just music here – there's outdoor theatre, comedy shows and even a cinema. The music is OK, but they're mostly pop bands that my parents like. I would like to see my favourite bands!

Camp Bestival

Joe, 13

When? Four days in July or August

Big or small? Medium: 30,000 people, 100 bands

How much? Aged 10–12: £110; aged 13–17: £135; adult: £200

My family goes on holiday to Dorset for two weeks every summer and we always go to Camp Bestival. It's in a big park with a beautiful castle, and it's fun because every year they have a theme. This year, the theme is 'movies' so people dress up as characters from films. It's famous for dance music, but there are other bands, too. The only problem is the campsite – it's far from the festival, so you have to walk a lot!

1 **Read the introduction to the text and look at the pictures of the festivals. Which festival would you like to go to? Why?**

2 🔊 **6.16 Read and listen to the text. Match the descriptions to the festivals.**

1 Most beautiful place
2 Best for music
3 Best for activities

3 **Read the text again. Copy and complete the table with notes.**

	Freddie at Glastonbury	Maya at Deer Shed	Joe at Camp Bestival
Likes			
Doesn't like			

4 **Word Power** **Find five types of music in the text. What other types of music do you know? What is your favourite type of music?**
rock ...

5 **COMPARE CULTURES** **Discuss the questions in small groups.**

1 Are music festivals popular in your country?
2 Which is the most famous?
3 Do you go to music festivals?
4 What other types of festivals are there in your country?

6 **Work in pairs. Look at the pictures of the musicians in the fact files. Answer the questions.**

1 What type of music do they make?
2 Do you know any of their songs?
3 Who is your favourite?

7 🔊 **6.17 Work in pairs. Guess the correct options to complete the fact files. Listen and check.**

Now watch the culture video.

FAST FINISHER

Write sentences about the music and the musicians you like or don't like.
I like rock music. My favourite band is Foo Fighters. I don't like classical music ...

ARIANA GRANDE

- She was born in [1] *1993 / 1998.*
- Her favourite subject at school was [2] *Music / Science.*
- Her most famous song is called [3] *'Yes, please' / 'Thank U, Next'.*
- She has [4] *27 / 72* million followers on Twitter.
- She has [5] *two / six* dogs.

LIL NAS X

- He was born in [6] *1994 / 1999.*
- He played the [7] *trumpet / piano* at school.
- His most famous song is called [8] *'New City Street' / 'Old Town Road'.*
- The song was streamed [9] *143 / 14* million times in one week.
- He has two dogs. They're called [10] *1 and 2 / 7 and 9.*

BILLIE EILISH

- She was born in [11] *1999 / 2001.*
- Both her parents are [12] *actors / teachers.*
- Her most famous song is called [13] *'Bad Guy' / 'Good Guy'.*
- She has [14] *5 / 50* million followers on Instagram.
- She has a dog called [15] *Pepper / Tomato.*

Pen friends

WRITING An email

I can write an email.

1 **Look at the website. Answer the questions.**

1 What kind of website is it?
2 Would you like a pen friend?
3 Which person would you choose for a pen friend? Why?

Home | Log in

World Pen Friends

Connect with people all around the world

User: Sofia-Napoli   Age: 12
Nationality: Likes:

User: Pedro338   Age: 12
Nationality: Likes:

2 **Read an email from Charlotte. Who is the email to? Why do you think she wrote to this person?**

To: Pedro338
Subject: Pen friends

Hi, Pedro,

How are you? My name is Charlotte and I like your profile on *World Pen Friends*. Do you want to be pen friends with me?

I want to tell you about my life. I live in Bournemouth, in the UK. I play videogames every evening and my favourite game is *Fortnite*. I sometimes play it with people in different countries. I love music! I listen to dance music and I also listen to K-pop. I play the guitar and I play the violin, too. At the weekend, I meet my friends. We sometimes go shopping or we go to the beach. I like football, too, and my favourite team is Bournemouth.

Where do you live? What computer games do you play? What do you do at the weekend? I know you like football, but what is your favourite team? Are there any beaches near your house?

Write soon!

Bye, Charlotte

3 **Read Charlotte's email again. Answer the questions.**

1 Where does Charlotte live?
2 How often does she play videogames?
3 What is her favourite game?
4 What type of music does she like?
5 What musical instruments does she play?
6 What does she do at the weekend?

4 **Look at the Useful language. How do you say these expressions in your language?**

Useful language

Writing an email

Hi ... / Dear ...
How are you? / I hope you're well.
I want to tell you about ...
Write soon!
Bye / Take care

5 **Read the Look! box. Find examples of *too* and *also* in Charlotte's profile.**

Look! *too/also*

We use *too* or *also* to add information.
I like pop music, but I like rock, ***too****.*
I like pop music, but I ***also*** *like rock.*

6 **Copy and complete the sentences with the words in brackets.**

1 My sister watches TV and she watches online videos. (also)
2 We're brothers and we're best friends. (also)
3 My parents listen to a lot of podcasts, but they listen to music. (too)
4 I visit my friends at the weekend and I visit museums. (too)

7 **Write an email to a pen friend from the website. Follow the steps in the Writing plan.**

Writing plan

Prepare

› Choose which person you want to write to.
› Make notes about what you do in your free time.
› Think of questions you want to ask the person.

Write

› Write your email.
› Use the expressions from the **Useful language** box.
› Use *too* and *also* to add extra information.

Check

› Check your grammar: adverbs and expressions of frequency; *Wh-* questions.
› Check *too* and *also*.
› Check your spelling and punctuation.

W **Writing summary:** WB p.89
R **Review: Units 4–6** SB pp.102–103
P **Project: Units 4–6** SB pp.108–109
L **Literature: Units 4–6** SB pp.114–115
LS **Language summary: Unit 6** SB p.123

Skills and sport

7

Vocabulary: Abilities; Sports | **Grammar:** *can* and *can't*; *like/love/hate*; Object pronouns | **Speaking:** Shopping for sports clothes | **Writing:** An application

VOCABULARY Abilities

I can talk about my abilities.

1 7.1 **Match the abilities in the box with the pictures. Listen, check and repeat.**

cook dance draw drive play the drums ride a bike
ride a horse sing speak French swim

1 

2 

talented teens
Young people today have lots of skills

3 

4 

5 

6 

7 

8 

9 

10 

2 7.2 **Listen to the sounds and write the abilities in your notebook.**

3 Complete the questions with the correct verbs.

1 Do you ... songs in the shower?
2 Do you ... pictures in English class?
3 Do you ... the drums?
4 Do you ... French?
5 Do you ... dinner for your family?
6 Do you ... when you listen to music?
7 Do you ... a bike to school?
8 Do you ... in the sea?

4 Work in pairs. Ask and answer the questions in Exercise 3. If your partner says 'yes', find out how often he/she does it.

A: Do you sing songs in the shower?
B: Yes, I do.
A: How often do you do it?
B: I sing pop songs every morning!

5 Tell the class about your partner.

Eva sings pop songs in the shower every morning ...

David speaks French ...

Now watch the vlog.

FAST FINISHER

Write sentences about people in your family and the abilities they have.

My mum speaks French and Italian. My little brother plays the drums.

LS Language summary: Unit 7 SB p.124

Amazing abilities

READING

I can guess the meaning of new words.

Tweens with talents

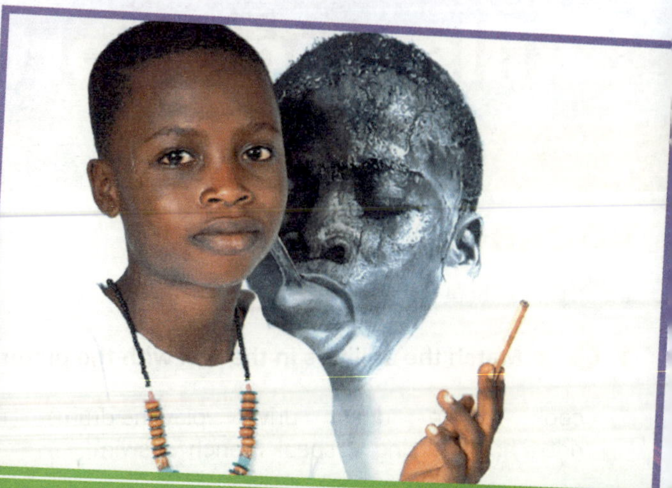

What [1] **talents** do you have? Are you a good singer or a good dancer? Can you cook? Can you speak French? Are you a fast swimmer or a good football player? Young people today can do amazing things!

Kareem Waris Olamilekan is an [2] **artist** and he draws beautiful pictures. He sees something and he can draw it perfectly! But there are some things he can't do ... for example, he can't drive. And he can't stay at home and draw pictures all day. Why? Because he goes to school – Kareem is only eleven! Kareem lives in Lagos, Nigeria with his family. We can't see his pictures in museums but they are on Instagram. And he's very [3] **popular** online – he has 154,000 followers!

Can you ride a bike? Can you ride a horse? Najiah Knight is a thirteen-year-old American girl and she can ride ... a bull! In the sport of bull-riding, riders try to stay on the bull for eight seconds. Sometimes they can do it, but sometimes they can't. When bull-riders [4] **fall** on the floor, they run ... fast! Najiah can't ride the very big bulls because she's too young, but she rides small bulls and these bulls can [5] **hurt** people, too. Najiah isn't [6] **scared**, she wants to be the best bull-rider in the world!

1 7.3 **Read and listen to the article. What is special about Kareem and Najiah?**

2 Read the article again. Copy and complete the sentences.

1 Kareem is ... years old.
2 He's from ... .
3 People see Kareem's pictures ... .
4 Najiah is ... years old.
5 She's from ... .
6 She doesn't ride ... bulls because she's young.

3 Look at the words in bold in the article. Answer the questions to help you understand them.

1 Are the words nouns, verbs or adjectives?
2 Are there similar words in your language?

4 Word Power Find words for the people who do the verbs in the box. Do you know any other words for people ending in *-er*?

dance	play	ride	sing	swim

5 FIND OUT Bobby Fischer was a chess player. He won a famous game in 1956. It was called 'The Game of the Century'. How old was Fischer in 1956?

FUN FACT

We all know Justin Bieber can sing, dance and play instruments. But he has other talents, too. He can speak two languages (English and French) and he can solve a Rubik's Cube in under two minutes!

GRAMMAR *can*: affirmative and negative

I can use *can* to talk about ability.

Now watch the grammar animation.

1 **Read the grammar box. Choose the correct answers to complete the rules.**

Affirmative	I/You/He/She/It **can** speak four languages. We/You/They **can** drive a car.
Negative	I/You/He/She/It **can't** sing. We/You/They **can't** speak Spanish.

Rules

The verb *can* [1] *changes / doesn't change* when the subject is *he, she* or *it*.

After *can*, we use a verb [2] *with to / without to*.

2 **Copy and complete the sentences with *can* or *can't*.**

1 I ... play the drums. (✓)
2 My mum ... swim. (✗)
3 I ... draw animals. (✓)
4 My dad ... drive. (✗)
5 I ... speak Spanish. (✓)
6 My best friend ... sing! (✗)

3 **Rewrite the sentences from Exercise 2 so they are true for you.**

I can't play the drums.

can: questions and short answers

I can use questions with *can* to ask about abilities.

4 **Read the grammar box. Choose the correct answers to complete the rules.**

Questions	Short answers
Can you drive?	Yes, I **can**. / No, I **can't**.
Can they speak French?	Yes, they **can**. / No, they **can't**.

Rules

In questions, *can* comes [1] *before / after* the subject.

In short answers we use [2] *do or don't / can or can't.*

5 **PRONUNCIATION** ***can* and *can't***

7.4 **Listen to the pronunciation of *can* and *can't*. Listen again and repeat.**

/kən/	/kæn/	/kɑːnt/
Can you drive? I **can** speak French.	Yes, I **can**.	No, I **can't**. My mum **can't** swim.

6 **Put the words in the correct order to make questions.**

1 Kareem / can / drive / ?
2 ride / a bull / Najiah / can / ?
3 dad / can / drive / your / ?
4 mum / ride / your / a horse / can / ?
5 play / you / can / the guitar / ?
6 cook / you / can / ?

7 **Work in pairs. Ask and answer the questions in Exercise 6.**

8 **Copy the table in your notebook. Find people in your class with the abilities. Ask questions to find extra information.**

Ability		Name and extra information
1 	Can you play an instrument? Which instrument can you play?	
2 	Can you sing a song in English? Which song is it?	
3 	Can you cook a meal? What do you usually cook?	
4 	Can you swim? How far can you swim?	
5 	Can you ride a horse? How often do you do it?	
6 	Can you say 'hello' in five languages? How do you say the words?	

9 **Work in pairs. Use your tables to talk about your classmates.**

Enrique can swim for 1 km.

FAST FINISHER

Write sentences about famous people's abilities. Use *can* and *can't*.

Usain Bolt can run 100m in 9.58 seconds.

LS Language summary: Unit 7 SB p.124

I love it!

VOCABULARY and LISTENING Sports

I can listen for people's opinions.

1 7.5 **Match the sports with the pictures. Listen, check and repeat.**

athletics baseball basketball climbing football gymnastics
martial arts mountain biking running skateboarding skiing tennis

2 7.6 **Read the Look! box. Copy and complete the table with the sports from Exercise 1. Listen, check and repeat.**

Look! *play, go and do*

We use **play** with ball sports: e.g. *I **play** basketball.*
We use **go** with sports ending in *-ing*:
e.g. *I **go** running.*
We use **do** with other sports: e.g. *I **do** martial arts.*

play	go	do
basketball	*running*	*martial arts*

3 **Work in pairs. Say which sports you do and how often you do them? Are there any sports you only watch on TV?**

I play football three times a week.

I watch athletics on TV.

4 7.7 **Listen to five people talking about sports. Copy and complete the table with their favourite sports and write if they do the sport, watch it or both.**

	Favourite sport	Do / Watch / Both
Lola		
Briony		
Ed		
Mia		
Jack		

5 7.7 **Listen again. Match the speakers' opinions with the activities.**

1 **Lola:** running programmes
2 **Briony:** skateboarders
3 **Ed:** skiing
4 **Mia:** Nick Kyrgios
5 **Jack:** baseball

a expensive
b exciting
c boring
d great
e cool

LS Language summary: Unit 7 SB p.124

GRAMMAR *like/love/hate*

I can give my opinion of activities.

Now watch the grammar animation.

1 **Read the grammar box. Complete the rules with *like, not like, love* and *hate*.**

I **love** running – I go running three times a week.

I **like** a lot of sports, but my favourite is skiing.

I **don't like** many sports.

I **hate** football – it's so boring!

Rules

😍 [1] ... ☹️ [3] ...

🙂 [2] ... 😡 [4] ...

2 **Copy and complete the sentences about the five people from Exercise 5 on page 72.**

1 Lola ... 😍 running, but she ... ☹️ running programmes.

2 Briony ... 🙂 skateboarding and she ... 😍 skateboarders.

3 Ed ... 🙂 a lot of sports and he ... 😍 skiing.

4 Mia's sister ... 🙂 tennis, but she ... ☹️ Nick Kyrgios.

5 Jack ... ☹️ basketball or tennis and he ... 😡 football.

3 **Write sentences with *like, not like, love* and *hate* about the sports on page 72.**

I like running and athletics, but I love gymnastics!

Object pronouns

I can use object pronouns.

4 **Read the sentences. Complete the grammar box.**

I don't go skateboarding. I can't do **it**!

I play tennis with my sister. I often beat **her**.

My favourite player is Nick Kyrgios, but my sister doesn't like **him**.

I sometimes watch baseball and my friends watch it with **me**.

Singular		Plural	
Subject pronoun	Object pronoun	Subject pronoun	Object pronoun
I	[1] ...	we	**us**
you	**you**	you	**you**
he	[2] ...	they	**them**
she	[3] ...		
it	[4] ...		

5 7.8 **Copy and complete Ben's email with the correct object pronouns. Listen and check.**

To: Daisy

Subject: Favourite sport

Hi Daisy!

I want to tell [1] ... about my favourite sport – climbing. I love [2] ... because it's exciting. I go to the climbing centre every week with Tara. I go with [3] ... because she's my best friend. Our teacher at the climbing centre is called John. We like [4] ... because he teaches [5] ... a lot. After the lesson, John and the other teachers climb the big wall and we watch [6] ... . The big wall is very difficult, but they can climb [7] ... in 5 minutes! Do you want to come with me and learn to climb? I can teach [8] ...!

Write soon!

Bye,

Ben

6 **In your notebook, write an example for each topic.**

a sportsperson

Coco Gauff

a sports team

an actor

a music group

a singer

a TV programme

a type of food

7 **Work in pairs. Ask and answer *What do you think of ...?* for your partner's examples.**

A: What do you think of Coco Gauff?

B: I love her. She's a great tennis player!

FAST FINISHER

Write sentences about things you love and things you hate.

I hate Mondays, but I love the weekend.

LS Language summary: Unit 7 SB p.124

KEEP TALKING!

Can I help you?

READING and LISTENING

I can understand a shopping website.

1 **Look at the pictures on the website. Match the products with the sports.**

1 running
2 mountain biking
3 football
4 swimming

2 **Read the information about the products. Copy and complete the table.**

	Price	Colours	Sizes	Reviews
helmet	£8.99	1 ...	2 ...	3.5 / 5
goggles	3 ...	white, blue, yellow	4 ...	4.5 / 5
football kit	£24.50	5 ...	XS, S, M, L	6 ... / 5
trainers	7 ...	blue, green, black	36–40	8 ... / 5

3 7.9 **Listen to Matt and Erin. Which products from the website do they talk about?**

4 7.9 **Listen again and choose the correct answers.**

1 Matt wants to buy a birthday present for *Poppy / Erin*.
2 Matt doesn't buy a helmet because Poppy *can't ride a bike / has a helmet*.
3 Poppy *never / sometimes* goes running with her dad.
4 Matt doesn't buy the trainers because *he doesn't know her size / they have bad reviews*.
5 Poppy's favourite colour is *blue / green*.
6 Poppy's birthday is on *Tuesday / Wednesday*.

5 THINK CRITICALLY **Work in pairs. Do you buy things in shops or do you shop online? What are the advantages and disadvantages of shopping online?**

SPEAKING Shopping for sports clothes

I can buy something in a shop.

1 7.10 **Listen and read. Is the football kit cheaper or more expensive than on the website?**

Assistant: Hello, can I help you?
Matt: Do you have any football kits?
Assistant: Yes, we do. They're over there next to the shoes. Which size do you want?
Matt: I'd like medium, please.
Assistant: The medium kits are here.
Matt: Thanks. Do you have it in green?
Assistant: Yes, we do. Here's a medium football kit in green.
Matt: Perfect. How much is it?
Assistant: It's £22.50.
Matt: That's great! I'll take it.
Assistant: No problem. Do you want anything else?
Matt: No, thanks, just the football kit.

2 7.11 **Listen and repeat the Useful language.**

Useful language

Shopping for sports clothes

Shop assistant	Customer
Can I help you?	Do you have any ...?
They're over there.	I'd like small/medium/large, please.
The ... are here.	Do you have it/them in ...?
Which size/colour do you want?	How much is it / are they?
I'm sorry. We don't have any.	I'll take it/them.
It's / They're ten pounds.	

3 7.12 **Copy and complete the dialogue. Listen and check.**

Assistant: Good morning. Can I [1] ... you?
Customer: Do you [2] ... any running socks?
Assistant: Yes, we do. They're over [3] ... . Which [4] ... do you want?
Customer: I'd [5] ... small, please.
Assistant: The small running socks are here.
Customer: Do you have [6] ... in blue?
Assistant: I'm sorry. We don't have [7] ... .
Customer: OK. I'll [8] ... the white socks. How [9] ... are they?
Assistant: [10] ... £2.50. Do you want anything else?
Customer: No, thanks, just the socks.

4 **Work in pairs. Prepare a new dialogue in a sports shop. Follow the steps in the Speaking plan.**

Speaking plan

Prepare

- Decide on your roles.
- Choose a product from the website on page 74.
- Make notes for your dialogue.

Speak

- Practise your dialogue.
- Use phrases from the **Useful language** box.
- Act out your dialogue without notes.

Reflect

- How can you improve next time?
- Swap roles and choose a different item from the website.

Now play *Keep moving!*

FAST FINISHER

Write a dialogue in a shop for a different product.

A: Hello. Can I help you?
B: Do you have any pencil cases?

REAL CULTURE!

The Scouts

I can compare youth groups in the UK with groups in my country.

How many badges can you get?

In the UK, there's an organization called the Scouts. Young people meet together and try new activities, learn new skills and have adventures. Many of the activities are outside and Scouts often go camping or walking in the countryside. Scouts are aged 10½ to 14 years old, but there are other groups for younger children, too. Altogether there are 639,000 young people in the Scouts in the UK. When Scouts learn a new skill, they get a badge and they wear the badge on their uniform. There are 75 badges you can get. Here are four popular ones:

1 ... activity badge

Can you read a map? Do you like them? For this badge you need to:

- find places on a map.
- use the map in an activity.
- draw a map.

2 ... activity badge

Do you like skateboarding? What about parkour – can you do that? For this badge you need to:

- choose a street sport and improve your skills.
- show that you can do the sport in a safe way.

3 ... activity badge

Do you have a camera? Can you take good photos? For this badge you need to:

- take some black-and-white photos of people, animals and objects.
- show your photos to other people and describe them.

4 ... activity badge

Do you like computers? For this badge you need to:

- show you understand computers.
- find information online.
- use the information to give a presentation.

1 🔊 7.13 **Read the introduction to the article. Match the names of the badges with descriptions 1–4. Read and listen to the article. Check your answers.**

Digital citizen   Navigator   Photographer   Street sports

2 Read the article again. Are the sentences true (T) or false (F)?

1 Camping and walking are popular activities in the Scouts.
2 Scouts are for children and adults.
3 Scouts put their badges on their clothes.
4 Skateboarders can get the Street sports activity badge.
5 To get the Photographer activity badge, you can only take photos of people.
6 The Digital citizen activity badge is about playing videogames.

3 Word Power Look at the blue words in the article. Complete the questions with the correct words.

1 How often do you use a ...?
2 How often do you walk in the ...?
3 Do you like having ...?
4 Do you prefer being inside or ...?

4 Work in pairs. Ask and answer the questions from Exercise 3.

5 🔊 7.14 **Listen to three Scouts talking about the badges they want to get and match them to the badges.**

6 Work in pairs. Ask and answer the questions.

1 Which badges are fun?
2 Which badges are useful?
3 Which badges are easy?
4 Which badge would you like to get most?

7 COMPARE CULTURES Work in pairs and ask and answer the questions.

1 Are there Scouts in your country?
2 Are they similar to Scouts in the UK?
3 Are there other organizations for young people in your country?
4 What skills do young people like learning in your country?

8 GET CREATIVE Work in pairs. Design a new activity badge for the Scouts.

1 Choose a skill or activity.
2 Write a list of what you need to do for this badge.
3 Draw a picture of your badge.

FUN FACT

Scouts are usually young, but not always. This is Ray Aldous – at 85 years old, he is Britain's oldest Scout leader! He says he likes it because it keeps him healthy.

Now watch the culture video.

FAST FINISHER

Imagine you are taking one of the Scout badges from this lesson. Write sentences about the things you do.

I want to take the Chef badge. I can cook lasagne ...

My skills and interests

WRITING An application

I can write an application for a summer camp.

1 Read the online application for a summer camp. What does Jorge write about?

a his family
b his hobbies
c his skills
d food he wants to eat
e new activities he wants to do

ADVENTURE CAMP UK

HAVE AN ADVENTURE AND LEARN ENGLISH IN THE UK

User: Jorge Perez

Application: 50% complete

Camp details ✓ Personal details ✓
Personal statement ☐ Payment ☐

Please tell us about your interests, abilities and the activities you want to do at camp, so we can put you in a suitable group:

I like a lot of sports, but my favourite sport is basketball – I'm very good at it and I play in the school basketball team. I also play baseball and football. I don't like tennis and I think it's quite boring. I can swim well and I like all water sports. I can ride a bike, but I can't ride a horse.

I'm from Spain and I speak Spanish. I study English at school and I can speak English well. I watch films in English and I read books in English, too. I can also speak French a little, but I'm not very good at it. I love music. I listen to rock and pop music. I can play the drums and the guitar and I sometimes sing my favourite songs with my guitar.

At camp, I want to try new activities. I'd like to go climbing and do martial arts, like karate or judo – I think they're really exciting. I'd also like to speak to English children my age and make friends with them.

2 Read the text again. Are the sentences true (T) or false (F)?

1 Jorge is good at basketball.
2 He likes swimming.
3 He reads books in French.
4 He can play pop songs on his guitar.
5 He wants to ride a horse at camp.
6 He wants to meet Spanish children.

3 Look at the Useful language box. How do you say these sentences in your language?

Useful language

Interests and abilities

My favourite sport is ...
I like/don't like/hate/love ...
I think ... is fun/boring.
I'm (not) good at ...
I can/can't ... well.
I'd like to try ...

4 Read the Look! box. Find examples of *really*, *very*, *quite* and *not very* in the text.

Look! Modifiers

Modifiers make adjectives stronger or weaker.
*I'm **really/very** good at basketball.*
*I'm **quite** good at basketball.*
*I'm **not very** good at basketball.*

5 Add modifiers to the sentences to make them true for you.

1 I'm good at English.
2 Pop music is boring.
3 Swimming is fun.
4 My house is big.

6 Write an application for a summer camp. Follow the steps in the Writing plan.

Writing plan

Prepare

› Make a list of hobbies you like and don't like.
› Make a list of skills you have and things you can do.
› Think about which activities you would like to try.

Write

› Use your notes to complete the application.
› Use the expressions from the **Useful language** box.
› Use modifiers to make adjectives stronger or weaker.

Check

› Check your grammar: *can/can't*; *like/love/hate*; object pronouns.
› Check your use of modifiers.

W Writing summary WB p.90 **L Language summary: Unit 7** SB p.124

About town

8

Vocabulary: Places in a town; Adjectives to describe places | **Grammar:** Present continuous | **Speaking:** Directions | **Writing:** A text message

VOCABULARY Places in a town

I can describe my town.

1 8.1 **Match the places with the pictures. Listen, check and repeat.**

bank factory farm hospital hotel library market shop
sports centre supermarket swimming pool train station

Guess where the people are!

2 **Work in pairs. Ask and answer *Where do you …?* with the phrases in the box.**

borrow books buy a lot of food
buy clothes buy fruit and vegetables
catch a train get money make things
play tennis see a doctor see animals
sleep in a bed swim

A: Where do you borrow books?

B: In a library!

3 **Work in pairs. What places are there in your town?**

There's a library, but there isn't a factory.

4 **THINK CRITICALLY** **Work in small groups. Which are the five most important places for a town?**

I think a market is important, but you can buy more things in a supermarket.

Now watch the vlog.

FAST FINISHER

Write sentences about how often you go to different places in town.

I never go to the bank. I go to the swimming pool once a week.

LS **Language summary: Unit 8** **SB** p.125

Welcome to my town!

READING

I can understand the main ideas in a text.

What's On | Maps | Things to do

Bristol for Teens

Are you planning to visit Bristol? Do you want to know the best places to see? Lauren tells us about the perfect day in Bristol for people her age.

Hi, my name's Lauren and I'm British. I'm thirteen years old and I live in Bristol. Here's my perfect Saturday in the city.

1 Clifton Lido

It's 8.30 in the morning and some of my friends are getting up at this time ... but I'm swimming in this beautiful outdoor swimming pool. Well actually, I'm not swimming – I'm having breakfast at the café! The swimming pool is usually very busy, but if you come early in the morning there are only a few people here. A morning swim is a great way to start the day!

2 St Nicholas Market

Now it's 10.45 and I'm with some friends at this cool market. You can buy a lot of different things here – food, clothes, music, posters and jewellery. We're looking at the shops and we're listening to a musician – he's playing the guitar. He's really good and a lot of people are giving him money.

3 Harbourside

This is my favourite part of town. There are no shops, but there are a few cafés, museums, boats, a cinema ... and a lot of people! It's the afternoon now and some people are taking photos, but we're sitting next to the river and we're eating ice creams. It's a great place to hang out and chat with friends.

4 Cabot Tower

It's 5.00 in the afternoon and I'm climbing up the Cabot Tower. It's really quiet at the top and there are no people. I can see houses, parks, shops, the train station ... I can even see the hospital! My mum is a doctor there, but she isn't working today. The view is fantastic and it's a great way to end the day.

1 8.2 **Look at the pictures of Bristol in the UK. What places in a town do you think Lauren writes about? Read and listen to the text and check.**

2 Match the places with the activities. Read the text again and check.

1 Clifton Lido
2 St Nicholas Market
3 Harbourside
4 Cabot Tower

a look at the city
b meet friends
c go shopping
d do exercise

3 Word Power **Order the expressions from the text from smallest to the largest.**

a a few people
b some people
c a lot of people
d no people

4 Find more phrases with *a few, some, a lot of* and *no* in the text.

5 Work in pairs. Choose four places in your town to visit. What can you do there?

The sports centre is great. You can play tennis, football and basketball ...

GRAMMAR Present continuous: affirmative and negative

I can use the present continuous to talk about what is happening now.

Now watch the grammar animation.

1 Read the grammar box. Choose the correct answers to complete the rules.

Affirmative	Negative
I'**m getting** dressed.	I'**m not listening.**
You'**re visiting** Bristol.	You **aren't driving**.
He/She/It'**s running**.	He/She/It **isn't swimming**.
We/You/They'**re taking** photos.	We/You/They **aren't having** lunch.

Rules

In the present continuous, we use the verb [1] *be / do* and the main verb + *-ing*.

For verbs ending in *-e*, we [2] *remove / double* the *e* and add *-ing*.

For verbs ending in consonant-vowel-consonant, we [3] *remove / double* the final consonant and add *-ing*.

2 Write the *-ing* forms of the verbs. Check your answers in the text on page 80.

1 plan *planning*
2 swim
3 get
4 have
5 look
6 listen
7 give
8 take
9 eat
10 climb

3 PRONUNCIATION *-ing* sound

8.3 Listen and repeat the *-ing* form of the verbs.

1 making
2 running
3 playing
4 working
5 sitting
6 going

4 8.4 Say the *-ing* forms of the verbs in Exercise 2. Listen and repeat.

5 Copy and complete the sentences with the present continuous form of the verbs in brackets.

1 We ... (not go) to school. We ... (go) shopping!
2 My dad ... (drive) to work. He ... (not take) the train.
3 My mum ... (sleep). She ... (not work) today.
4 My cousins ... (not swim). They ... (run) in the park.
5 I ... (not have) breakfast. I ... (do) my homework!
6 You ... (not walk) to school. You ... (ride) your bike.
7 He ... (not take) photos. He ... (chat) with his friends.
8 They ... (listen) to a musician at the market. They ... (not buy) fruit and vegetables.

6 Work in pairs. Look at pictures A and B. Find six differences.

A: Hannah is wearing jeans in picture A.

B: Hannah isn't wearing jeans in picture B. She's wearing a skirt.

A

B

FAST FINISHER

Write sentences about what your friends and family are doing and what they aren't doing now.

Marco isn't playing videogames. He's studying English.

LS Language summary: Unit 8 SB p.125

What are you doing?

VOCABULARY and LISTENING Adjectives to describe places

I can understand phone conversations.

1 8.5 **Complete the descriptions with the adjectives in the box. Listen, check and repeat.**

clean	crowded	dangerous	dirty	empty	horrible	new	nice	noisy	old	quiet	safe

1 a ... road

2 a ... road

3 a ... building

4 an ... building

5 a ... shop

6 an ... shop

7 a ... place

8 a ... place

9 a ... classroom

10 a ... classroom

11 a ... park

12 a ... park

2 **Work in pairs. Think of examples of the places in the box. Which adjectives can you use to describe them?**

a building	a market	a park
a restaurant	a shop	a street

A: Luigi's is a nice restaurant.
B: Yes, it's clean and quiet.

3 8.6 **Look at the picture and read the messages. What adjectives can you use to describe Chatuchak market and some of the things in it? Listen to the conversation and check.**

4 8.6 **Listen again. Are the sentences true (T) or false (F)?**

1 The market is busy.
2 Monica's brother and dad are eating fruit.
3 Monica's dad is buying a T-shirt.
4 The music is coming from a clothes stall.
5 Monica is giving money to some street performers.
6 The street performers are playing music.

LS Language summary: Unit 8 SB p.125

GRAMMAR Present continuous: questions and short answers

I can ask and answer questions using the present continuous.

Now watch the grammar animation.

1 **Read the grammar box. In present continuous questions, does *be* come *before* or *after* the subject?**

Questions	Short answers
Are you **eating** something?	Yes, I **am**. / No, I**'m not**.
Is he **buying** something?	Yes, he **is**. / No, he **isn't**.
Are they **playing** music?	Yes, they **are**. / No, they **aren't**.

2 **Put the words in the correct order to make present continuous questions.**

1 you and Sarah / meeting / at the park / are / ?
2 to the library / going / are / you / ?
3 Zoe / walking / with you / is / ?
4 shopping / you / in the market / are / ?
5 buying / are / a new flat / your parents / ?
6 your phone / is / ringing / ?

3 8.7 **Match the answers with the questions in Exercise 2. Listen and check.**

a Yes, I am. It's really busy!
b No, it isn't. I think it's your phone!
c Yes, they are. It's really lovely!
d Yes, we are. Do you want to come?
e No, she isn't. She's at the station with her mum.
f No, I'm not. I'm going to the beach.

4 **Read the Look! box. Copy and complete the questions with *What, Where, Why, Who*.**

Look! ***Wh-* questions with the present continuous**

We put question words before *am/is/are* to make *Wh*-questions in the present continuous.

1 '... are you eating?' 'A sandwich.'
2 '... is Joe going?' ' To his guitar lesson.'
3 '... is winning the match?' 'Real Madrid.'
4 '... are they running?' 'Because they're late!'

5 **Write present continuous questions about Monica's visit to the market.**

Monica's dad and brother / have a snack / ?
Are Monica's dad and brother having a snack?

1 what / they / eat / ?
2 Monica's mum / buy something / ?
3 what / she / look at / ?
4 where / the music / come from / ?
5 Monica / give money to the street performers / ?
6 the street performers / sing / ?
7 what / they / do / ?

6 **Work in pairs. Ask and answer the questions in Exercise 5.**

A: Are Monica's dad and brother having a snack?
B: Yes, they are.

7 8.8 **Look at the picture. What is the boy doing? Listen and check.**

8 **Work in pairs. Act out activities from the box. Can your partner guess what you are doing?**

cook a pizza dance do homework drive a car eat an ice cream go shopping have a shower play baseball play the guitar read a book ride a bike ride a horse run swim watch TV

A: Are you riding a bike?
B: No, I'm not! Guess again!

9 **FIND OUT** ***The Harvesters*** **is a famous painting by Pieter Bruegel the Elder. Find a picture of the painting. What are the people doing?**

FAST FINISHER

Write a text message to a friend on holiday.

Hi Juan, how is your holiday? What are you doing?

LS **Language summary: Unit 8** **SB** p.125

KEEP TALKING!

Is the skatepark near here?

READING and LISTENING

I can find places on a town map.

1 **Look at a map of Larchester. Which places are there in the town?**
There are shops ...

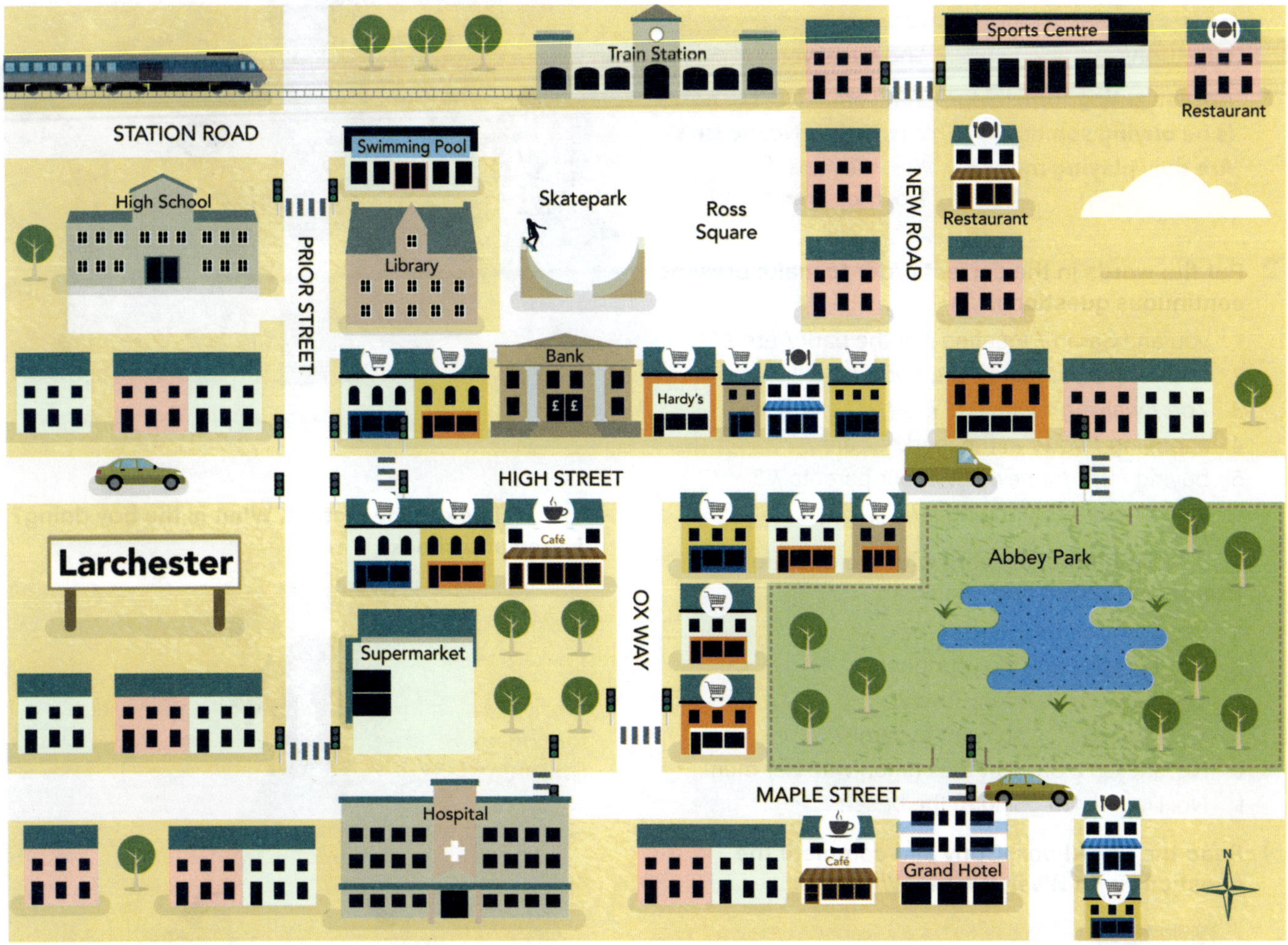

2 **Read the Look! box. Copy and complete the sentences with the prepositions in the box.**

Look! ***in front of / opposite***

*The red car is **in front of** the blue car.*

*The red car is **opposite** the blue car.*

behind	in front of	next to	opposite

1 The traffic lights are ... the supermarket.
2 There's a café ... the hotel.
3 The train station is ... the skatepark.
4 There's a park ... the hotel.

3 **8.9 Listen to a dialogue between Abigail, a new student at Larchester High School, and her classmate Nathan. Which places do they talk about?**

4 **8.9 Listen again. Copy and complete the sentences. Then check with a partner.**

1 Abigail wants to buy some ... .
2 The market is every ... .
3 There's a new clothes shop next to ... .
4 There's a nice café next to ... .
5 The sports centre is crowded at the ... .
6 The skatepark is ... the library.

SPEAKING Directions

I can ask for and give directions.

1 8.10 **Listen and read. Where is Abigail going?**

Abigail: Excuse me, I'm looking for the skatepark. Is it near here?
Boy: Yes, it is.
Abigail: Great. How do you get there?
Boy: OK – this is Prior Street. You go straight on, and you go past the library and the swimming pool.
Abigail: The library and the swimming pool.
Boy: Then you turn right onto Station Road.
Abigail: Station Road, OK.
Boy: Then you turn right again and the skatepark is in front of you. It's next to Ross Square.
Abigail: Is it far?
Boy: No – just five minutes.
Abigail: Thank you very much.
Boy: No problem.

2 8.11 **Listen and repeat the Useful language.**

Useful language

Asking for directions	Giving directions
Excuse me, ...	(Then) you go straight on.
I'm looking for ...	You turn right/left.
Is there a ... near here?	You go past the ...
Is it far? / Is it near here?	It's in front of / next to ...
How do you get there?	

3 Look at the pictures. Copy and complete the directions.

1 You turn ... .

2 Then go ... on.

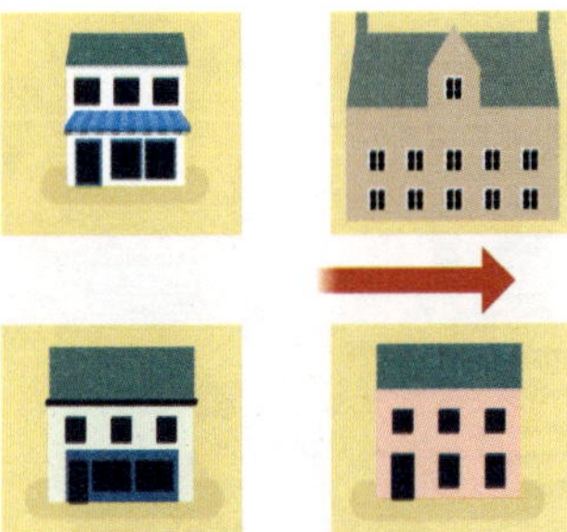

3 You go ... the library.

4 It's ... the café.

4 8.12 **Abigail is outside the hotel on Maple Street. Listen to the dialogues and look at the map on page 84. Match the places with the dialogues.**

bank restaurant school supermarket

1 ... 2 ... 3 ... 4 ...

5 Work in pairs. Prepare another dialogue asking for and giving directions. Follow the steps in the Speaking plan.

Speaking plan

Prepare

- Decide on your roles.
- Use the map of Larchester on page 84. Choose where you are and where you want to go.
- Make notes for your dialogue.

Speak

- Practise your dialogue.
- Use phrases from the **Useful language** box.
- Act out your dialogue without notes.

Reflect

- How can you improve next time?
- Swap roles. Choose two new places and ask for directions.

Now play *Keep moving!*

FAST FINISHER

Think of places near your school. Write directions.

(The library) You leave school and you turn right. Then you go past the supermarket ...

LS **Language summary: Unit 8** SB p.125

REAL CULTURE!

Street party!

I can compare local events in the UK with my country.

Home Posts About Search

The Big Lunch

The Big Lunch started in 2009 and it happens every year in the UK. On one weekend of the year, people around the UK meet and have lunch together. The lunches are often in people's streets, but they can be anywhere: in schools, libraries, parks – even on the beach! Communities come together and talk, make new friends and eat delicious food!

Each year, there are thousands of 'big lunches' in the UK and over 6 million people take part. But a *Big Lunch* is not just about food – there are lots of other fun activities to get to know people. Here are some pictures of people at *Big Lunch* events around the country.

Brighton

These children in Brighton are painting the road! They're drawing pictures and writing messages to people. There's paint everywhere! But don't worry – it's easy to clean after the party.

London

This street in London is usually very quiet, but today everything is different. There are balloons, tables, food and there's even a dog show! People are walking their dogs down the street and the dogs are doing tricks. The neighbours are clapping and giving each dog a score out of ten.

Nottingham

These children are playing a game called 'tug of war'. There are two teams – one team is pulling the rope *up* the street, the other team is pulling it *down* the street. Tug of war is hard work!

Windsor

These women are having an 'egg and spoon race'. It's like a normal race, but everybody is holding an egg on a spoon. They're being careful because they don't want the egg to fall. Broken eggs are very messy!

8

1 8.13 **Look at the pictures on the website about *The Big Lunch*. What are the people doing? Read and listen to the text. Check your answers.**

2 **Choose the correct options to answer the questions. Read the text again and check.**

1 What is *The Big Lunch*?
  a an outdoor café
  b a party
  c a cookery school
2 Why do people take part in *The Big Lunch*?
  a Because they sell food there.
  b Because they learn to cook there.
  c Because they meet people there.
3 What are the children in Brighton doing?
  a They're painting the road.
  b They're cleaning the road.
  c They're playing in the road.
4 What is the street in London usually like?
  a crowded
  b dangerous
  c quiet
5 How many teams are there for tug of war?
  a one
  b two
  c three
6 Why are the women in Windsor being careful?
  a Because the eggs can break.
  b Because the game is dangerous.
  c Because they want to win the race.

3 **Word Power** **Look at the blue words in the text. Match them with the definitions.**

1 everywhere	a all the people
2 everything	b all the places
3 everybody	c all the things

4 **Copy and complete the sentences with the words from Exercise 3. Which sentences are true for you?**

1 I want to go ... in the world.
2 I know ... on my street.
3 I eat ...!

5 **COMPARE CULTURES** **Work in pairs. Ask and answer the questions.**

1 Do you know your neighbours well?
2 Are there street parties in your town?
3 What happens at the street parties?
4 What other events do you have in your local area?

6 **GET CREATIVE** **Work in small groups. You are organizing a *Big Lunch* party. Discuss the questions. Make a poster for the party and show the class.**

- Where and when is the party?
- What food and drink is there?
- Who do you invite?
- What activities are there?

7 8.14 **Look at the pictures of other local projects. How do you think they help people in the community? Listen and match them to the descriptions.**

a

b

c

FUN FACT

This is the second biggest carnival in the world. 2.5 million people come every year to dance, eat and listen to the music, but it's not in Brazil ... it's in Notting Hill in London, in the UK.

Now watch the culture video.

FAST FINISHER

Imagine you are at a local event in your town. Write a description of what you can see.

A band is playing music and people are dancing in the street ...

Where do you want to meet?

WRITING A text message

I can write messages to make arrangements.

1 **Read the conversation between Jay and Tilly. Answer the questions.**

1 What are Jay and Tilly doing now?
2 What do they agree to do later?
3 Where and when do they agree to meet?

2 **Read the Look! box. Find examples of *right now* and *at the moment* in the text messages.**

Look! ***right now / at the moment***

We use *right now* and *at the moment* to talk about actions happening now.
At the moment*, I'm reading an interesting book.*
I'm playing computer games ***right now****.*

3 **Work in pairs. Say what your family is doing now. Use *right now* and *at the moment*.**

Right now, my brother is playing football.

4 **Read the Useful language. How do you say these expressions in your language?**

Useful language

Arranging to meet

Do you want to ...?
Where/When do you want to meet?
Let's meet at ... / Shall we meet at ...?
Can we meet at ... instead?
See you (there) at ...

5 **Work in pairs. Write a text message conversation and arrange to meet. Follow the steps in the Writing plan.**

Writing plan

Prepare

› Decide who sends the first message.
› Think about what you are doing now.

Write

› Greet your partner and ask what he/she is doing.
› Suggest an activity.
› Agree on a time and place to meet.
› Use the expressions from the **Useful language** box.
› Use *right now* and *at the moment*.

Check

› Check your grammar: present continuous.
› Check your punctuation is correct.
› Check your spelling.

FAST FINISHER

Write a text message between two famous people arranging to meet.

A: *Hi, Rosalia, what are you doing?*
B: *Hello, Beyoncé. I'm recording a song at the moment.*

Travel

9

Vocabulary: Weather and nature; Transport | **Grammar:** *be*: past simple; *be going to* | **Speaking:** Buying a train ticket | **Writing:** A review

VOCABULARY Weather and nature

I can talk about weather and nature.

1 9.1 **Match the weather descriptions with pictures A–D. There are two for each picture. Listen, check and repeat.**

It's cloudy. It's cold. It's hot. It's raining. It's snowing. It's sunny. It's warm. It's windy.

2 9.2 **Match the words with the natural features 1–8.**

beach field flower forest lake mountain sea tree

3 9.3 **Work in pairs. Describe the photos. Listen and compare with your descriptions.**

1 A man is walking on a beach. It's raining and it's windy ...

4 **Read the Look! box. Work in pairs. Answer the questions.**

> **Look!** ***rain* and *snow***
>
> *Rain* and *snow* are verbs. We use the present continuous to talk about the weather now.
>
> *It's **raining** right now. It **isn't snowing** at the moment.*
>
> We use the present simple to talk about the weather in general.
>
> *It never **rains** in summer. It sometimes **snows** in winter.*

1 What's the weather like now?
2 What's the weather usually like in spring/summer/autumn/winter?

Now watch the vlog.

FAST FINISHER

Write about the natural features near your town and what you can do there.

There's a forest and you can ride your bike ...

LS Language summary: Unit 9 SB p.126

It was a great holiday!

READING

I can compare texts.

Camping World

Tell us about your best and worst camping holidays. Where were you? Who were you with? Was the weather good?

I want to tell you about two camping holidays. My first camping holiday was 30 years ago and it wasn't good. I was thirteen years old and I was with my sister and my parents. We were in France and the weather was very bad. The campsite was in a forest and there was a beach nearby, but it was cold and windy, so we were in the tent every day and I was really bored! Our tent was small and there weren't any beds. I remember there were only two showers and they weren't clean ... and the water was cold! It was horrible!

Now, I'm 45 and I have two teenage sons, and they want to go camping. So last year we were in Italy on a camping holiday and it was very different. The weather was really good. It was sunny every day, but it wasn't too hot. There wasn't a beach, but the campsite was near a beautiful lake in the mountains. We weren't in a normal tent, we were in a big 'yurt' and there were real beds inside. There were clean showers and the water was warm. It was lots of fun and we want to go again soon.

Andy Hill

1 **Look at the pictures. Work in pairs. Ask and answer the questions.**

1 Do you go camping?
2 What are the good things about camping?
3 What are the bad things about camping?

2 9.4 **Read and listen to the article about two camping holidays. Match the pictures with Andy's holiday in France or Italy.**

3 **Read the article again. Complete the table comparing Andy's two holidays.**

	France	Italy
age	13	43
weather	1 ...	2 ...
nature	3 ...	4 ...
tent	5 ...	6 ...
showers	7 ...	8 ...

4 **Word Power** **Copy and complete the past time expressions from the article. How do you say the expressions in your language?**

Camping holiday in France: *30 years* 1 ...
Camping holiday in Italy: 2 *... year.*

5 **Complete the sentences with the correct days, months and years.**

1 Last year was ...
2 Three days ago was ...
3 Last month was ...
4 Ten years ago was ...

6 **FIND OUT** **Which countries are *yurts* from? Why do people in these countries use them?**

GRAMMAR *be*: past simple

I can talk about situations in the past.

1 **Read the grammar box. Complete the rules with *was, were, wasn't* and *weren't*.**

Affirmative	Negative
I **was** in France 30 years ago. We **were** near the beach.	Andy **wasn't** happy. They **weren't** in a normal tent.
Questions	**Short answers**
Were you with your family? **Was** the weather good?	Yes, I **was**. / No, I **wasn't**. Yes, it **was**. / No, it **wasn't**.

Rules
1 We use ... and ... with *I, he, she* and *it*.
2 We use ... and ... with *you, we* and *they*.

2 **Copy and complete the sentences with the affirmative (+) or negative (–) forms of *be* in the past simple.**
1 I ... happy yesterday. (+)
2 It ... cold and windy last week. (–)
3 My friends ... in the park yesterday. (+)
4 I ... hungry this morning. (+)
5 My grandparents ... at my house last weekend. (+)
6 Our teacher ... at school yesterday. (–)

3 **Which sentences from Exercise 2 are true for you? Compare with a partner.**

4 **PRONUNCIATION** ***was/wasn't***

9.5 **Listen and repeat.**
1 I **was** happy. I **wasn't** sad.
2 Where **was** Juan? He **wasn't** at school.
3 '**Was** it cold?' 'No, it **wasn't**.'

5 **Put the words in the correct order to make questions about Andy's two camping holidays.**
In France, ...
1 the holiday / good / was / ?
2 he / was / how old / ?
3 he / with his family / was /?
4 clean / were / the showers / ?
In Italy, ...
5 the holiday / how / was / ?
6 Andy's sons / were / with him / ?
7 a beach / the campsite / was / near / ?
8 was / cold / the water / ?

6 **Work in pairs. Ask and answer the questions from Exercise 5.**
A: Was the holiday in France good?
B: No, it wasn't.

7 **Read the Look! box. Change the sentences so they describe the past.**

Look! ***there was / there were***
We use *there was(n't)* for singular nouns and *there were(n't)* for plural nouns.
***There was** a lake, but **there wasn't** a beach.*
***There weren't** any normal tents, but **there were** big yurts.*

1 There's a supermarket and there are some shops in the town centre.
2 In the classroom, there isn't a computer and there aren't any books.
3 There are some mountains near us, but there isn't a lake.

8 9.6 **Look at the picture and listen to Emma talking about a holiday. Where was she?**

9 9.6 **Choose the correct words to answer the questions about Emma's holiday. Listen again and check.**
1 When was the holiday?
It was *last year / two months ago*.
2 Who was Emma with?
She was with *her friends / her family*.
3 Where were they?
They were in *a hotel / a campsite*.
4 What was there?
There was a beach and *mountains / some ruins*.
5 How was the weather?
It was *cold and windy / warm and sunny*.
6 Was it a good holiday?
Yes, it was. / No, it wasn't.

10 **Work in pairs. Think about a time when you were on holiday. Ask and answer questions about the holiday.**
A: When was the holiday?
B: It was last year.

FAST FINISHER
Choose some times in the past. Write sentences to say where you were.
At 6.30 a.m. I was in bed.

LS Language summary: Unit 9 SB p.126

On the move

VOCABULARY and LISTENING Transport

I can understand future plans.

1 9.7 **Match the types of transport with the pictures. Listen, check and repeat.**

bike boat bus car motorbike plane
scooter taxi train tram

1 

2 

3 

4 

5 

6 

7 

8 

9 

10 

2 **Work in pairs. Point at a type of transport. Can your partner remember the name?**

A: What's this?

B: It's a scooter.

3 **Work in pairs. Ask questions about types of transport and travel to places.**

How do you travel to ...?

How often do you travel by ...?

A: How do you travel to school?

B: I go by bike.

A: How often to you travel by tram?

B: I never travel by tram!

4 **Read the information about a podcast. How is the *Whole World School* different to your school?**

The *Whole World School* is different. Students from different countries travel the world and study together! They live and study in three different countries each year. Today we speak to a new student at the school, Gemma from the USA.

Listen

Download

5 9.8 **Listen to the podcast. Which three countries does Gemma plan to visit in her first year?**

Argentina Australia China
India Italy the USA

6 9.8 **Listen again. Copy and complete the table with Gemma's travel plans.**

Month	Country	Transport	Activities
January	1 ...	plane, train	cook Indian food, Indian music
April	2 ...	plane, 3 ...	4 ...
July	5 ...	6 ...	7 ...

FUN FACT

Graham Hughes is the first person to travel all around the world and **never** go by a plane! Instead, he travelled by cars, trains, buses, bikes ... and a lot of boats!

LS Language summary: Unit 9 SB p.126

GRAMMAR *be going to*: affirmative and negative

I can talk about future plans.

Now watch the grammar animation.

1 Read the grammar box. Choose the correct answer to complete the rule.

Affirmative	Negative
I**'m going to learn** about Indian music.	I**'m not going to study** English.
He/She**'s going to travel** by train.	He/She **isn't going to go** by bus.
We/You/They**'re going to see** some mountains.	We/You/They **aren't going to see** the sea.

Rule

We use *be* + *going to* + [1] *infinitive* / *-ing* form of the main verb to talk about future plans.

2 9.9 Copy and complete the text about Gemma's second year at the *Whole World School*. Use the affirmative (+) or negative (–) forms of *be going to*. Listen and check.

Next year, we [1]... (+) travel to France. I [2]... (–) stay in a hotel. I [3]... (+) stay with a French family. They [4]... (+) speak French to me every day, so I [5]... (+) learn a lot of French. Then, we [6]... (+) be in Japan for three months. I'm excited, but it [7]... (–) be easy for me. The food [8]... (+) be very different and it [9]... (–) be warm. In fact, I think it [10]... (+) snow!

3 Write affirmative and negative sentences about your plans for the times in the box.

after English class after school
tonight tomorrow

After English class, I'm going to have lunch.

I'm not going to play football tomorrow.

be going to: questions and short answers

4 Read the grammar box. Choose the correct answer to complete the rule.

Questions	Short answers
Are you **going to study** Maths?	Yes, I **am**. / No, I**'m not**.
Is she **going to go** back to the USA?	Yes, she **is**. / No, she **isn't**.
Are they **going to eat** Japanese food?	Yes, they **are**. / No, they **aren't**.

Rule

When we ask questions about future plans, the subject comes *before* / *after be*.

5 Write questions with *be going to* about Gemma's first year at the *Whole World School*.

1 when / she / travel to India / ?
2 she / travel / by car / ?
3 where / she / go / in April / ?
4 she / study / English / ?
5 how / she / travel to Argentina / ?
6 Gemma's parents / visit her / ?

6 Work in pairs. Ask and answer the questions about Gemma in Exercise 5.

A: When is she going to travel to India?

B: She's going to travel to India in January.

7 Work in pairs. Look at the pictures. Ask and answer questions about your plans for next summer.

A: Are you going to travel by plane?

B: No, I'm not.

travel by plane

go camping

swim in a swimming pool

play football

read a book

speak English

8 THINK CRITICALLY Work in small groups. Imagine you are planning a 'round-the-world trip'. Discuss the questions. Tell the class about your plans.

- Which countries are you going to visit?
- When are you going to go?
- How are you going to travel there?
- What are you going to do there?

FAST FINISHER

Choose a famous person. Write sentences about his/her plans for next week.

Bruno Mars is going to travel to New York for a concert ...

LS Language summary: Unit 9 SB p.126

KEEP TALKING!

A school trip

READING and LISTENING

I can understand information about a school trip.

Larkmead School Trip for Year 8 students

Friday

08.00 Travel to London by bus.

11.00 Arrive at Bridge View Hostel. Find rooms and leave bags.

12.00 Have lunch at the hostel café.

14.00 Visit the Natural History Museum. (3 hours)

17.30 Have dinner.

Saturday

08.30 Have breakfast at the hostel. Walk to the River Thames.

10.30 Travel along the river on City Cruise Boat. Have lunch on the boat. (3 hours)

14.00 Ride the London Eye and see the whole city.

16.00 Go to the Tate Modern art gallery by bike.

18.30 Eat fish and chips next to the river.

Sunday

08.30 Have breakfast at the hostel. Go by train to Baker Street.

10.00 Visit Madame Tussauds. Have lunch in Queen Mary's Rose Gardens.

14.00 Visit the British Museum. (2 hours)

15.00 Return to hotel. Travel back to school by bus.

18.00 Arrive at school.

1 **Does your school organize school trips? Where do you go? What do you do?**

2 **Look at the pictures. Where is the school trip to? Read the travel plans and check.**

3 **Read the text again. Answer the questions**

1 Where are the students going to stay in London?
2 How long are they going to be in the Natural History museum?
3 What time are they going to ride the London Eye?
4 How are they going to travel to the Tate Modern art gallery?
5 What are they going to have for dinner on Saturday?
6 Where are they going to visit on Sunday morning?

4 **What's your favourite day of the trip? Why? Compare with a partner.**

5 9.10 **Listen to Louisa and Joel talk about the plans for the school trip. Which places do they talk about?**

Madame Tussauds | The London Eye
The London Museum | The Natural History Museum
The river cruise | The Tate Modern

6 9.10 **Listen again. Answer the questions**

1 Which activity is Louisa excited about?
2 Does Louisa like museums?
3 Which museum has dinosaurs?
4 Where is Joel going to stay on Sunday night?
5 How is Joel going to travel home on Monday?

7 **GET CREATIVE** **Work in small groups. Think of a city you'd like to visit for a school trip. Write a plan for three days. Tell the class what you're going to do.**

We're going to visit Tokyo. On Friday morning at 8.00, we're going to travel by plane ...

SPEAKING Buying a train ticket

I can buy a ticket for public transport.

1 9.11 **Listen and read. How long is the journey from London to Birmingham?**

Assistant: Next, please.
Joel: Hi. I'd like a child ticket to Birmingham, please.
Assistant: Do you want a single or a return?
Joel: A single ticket, please.
Assistant: OK, that's £27.75, please.
Joel: Thanks. When is the next train to Birmingham?
Assistant: The next train leaves here at 10.15. It arrives at Birmingham New Street at 12.20.
Joel: OK, great. Where do I go?
Assistant: The train leaves from platform nine.
Joel: Platform nine.
Assistant: That's right. You go straight on and then turn right. Platform nine is opposite some shops.
Joel: OK, thanks very much.

2 9.12 **Listen and repeat the Useful language.**

Useful language

Buying a train ticket

Customer	Assistant
I'd like a (child) ticket to ..., please.	Do you want a single or a return?
A single/return ticket, please.	The next train leaves at ...
When is the next train to ...?	The train leaves from platform ...
Where do I go?	

3 9.13 **Copy and complete the dialogue. Listen and check.**

A: Hi. I'd like a [1]... to Oxford, please.
B: Do you want a [2]... or a return?
A: A [3]... ticket, please. I'm going to come back on Wednesday morning.
B: That's £12.50, please.
A: Here you are. When is the [4]... train to Oxford?
B: It [5]... at 11.15 and it arrives in Oxford at 12.05.
A: Thanks, and where do I [6]...?
B: The train leaves from [7]... four.

4 9.14 **Listen to two dialogues. Copy and complete the table.**

Destination	Ticket type	Cost	Time	Platform number
1 *Bristol*				
2				

5 Work in pairs. Have a dialogue where you buy a ticket on public transport. Follow the steps in the Speaking plan.

Speaking plan

Prepare

- Decide who is the customer and who is the ticket office assistant.
- Decide what type of public transport you're going to use.
- Make notes for your dialogue.

Speak

- Practise your dialogue.
- Use phrases from the **Useful language** box.
- Act out your dialogue without notes.

Reflect

- How can you improve next time?
- Swap roles and choose a different city and type of public transport.

Now play *Keep moving!*

FAST FINISHER

Write a dialogue between a ticket office assistant and a customer for your city.

Customer: *Hi. I'd like a ticket to ...*

LS Language summary: Unit 9 SB p.126

REAL CULTURE!

Famous transport

I can compare transport in my country with other countries.

THE BEAUTIFUL WAY TO TRAVEL

Sitting on the bus on your way to school is boring, but some cities have famous public transport systems. This week we're asking you to tell us about famous types of transport you're going to use in the holidays.

JASMINE

I'm on holiday in London. This afternoon I want to see all the famous buildings, but I'm not going to walk because it's raining. I'm going to catch a bus! London is famous for its double-decker buses – they have a downstairs and an upstairs! There are special buses for tourists, but they're expensive. I'm going to catch a normal bus and sit upstairs for the best views of the city!

TYLER

Look at all these yellow taxis. Can you guess where I am? I'm in New York, of course! But why are they yellow? It's because there aren't many yellow cars on the road, so it's easy to see a taxi if it's far away. There are more than 13,000 taxis in the city and 500,000 people use them every day! Tomorrow I'm going to go by taxi to the Empire State Building!

MATILDA

It was always my dream to ride a cable car in San Francisco, and tonight I'm going to do it – I'm really excited! Lots of cities have trams, but the first ones were in this city in 1873. I'm going to take a lot of photos, but I'm also going to hold on very tight. There are a lot of hills in San Francisco and the cable cars can sometimes go very fast!

CARLOS

Next week I'm going to be in Venice. There are no roads, so there are no cars, no scooters and no taxis. People travel around the city by boat and the most famous boats are gondolas. It's quite expensive – €80 for a trip, but six people can go together and I'm going to be there with five friends on my school trip – so it's perfect!

1 🔊 9.15 **Look at the pictures of types of transport. Guess which cities they are in. Read and listen to the article and check.**

2 Read the article again. Answer the questions.

1. What is the weather like in London?
2. Why isn't Jasmine going to go on the tourist bus?
3. Why are New York taxis yellow?
4. Where is Tyler going to visit tomorrow?
5. When were the first cable cars in San Francisco?
6. Do cable cars travel very fast?
7. Why are there no taxis in Venice?
8. How many people are going to be on Carlos's gondola?

3 Which of the types of transport would you like to try? Why?

4 **Word Power** **Look at the blue future time expressions in the article. How do you say them in your language?**

5 Work in pairs. Say what your plans are for the future times in the box.

next week	this afternoon	tomorrow	tonight

This afternoon I'm going to meet my friends.

6 🔊 9.16 **Look at some unusual types of transport from around the world. Match them with the countries in the box. Listen and check.**

China	Egypt	Philippines	Madeira

7 🔊 9.16 **Listen again and answer the questions about the types of transport.**

1. How many people can sit on a habal habal?
2. How far can the Maglev train travel in seven minutes?
3. Why do some people like travelling by felucca?
4. How do the drivers stop the Monte sledge?

8 **COMPARE CULTURES** **Work in pairs. Ask and answer the questions.**

1. Is there a lot of traffic in your city?
2. What types of public transport are there in your city?
3. What's the best way to travel for someone visiting your city?

Now watch the culture video.

FAST FINISHER

Are you going to travel somewhere soon? Write about your plans.

I'm going to go home on the bus this afternoon. The bus leaves at ...

1 Habal habal

2 Maglev train

3 Felucca

4 Monte sledge

Five stars!

WRITING A review

I can write an online review.

1 **Look at the picture of a theme park. Work in pairs. Answer the questions.**

1 Would you like to go on a ride like this?
2 Are there any theme parks near your city?
3 What are the good and bad things about theme parks?

2 **Read Roxy's review. How many stars do you think she gives *Stormworld*?**

Storm World

Good place, but very crowded!

Roxy: 18 August ☆ ☆ ☆ ☆ ☆

It was my birthday last Saturday, so I was at *Stormworld*. I was there with my family and some friends. I was very excited because I love theme parks.

There are a lot of good rides at *Stormworld*. The best ride is The Rattlesnake – it's really fast. I wasn't scared but my dad was! *Stormworld* is a very big theme park, but there's a small train to take people from one ride to another – I think that's a good idea.

However, there are some problems. It was really crowded, so there were long queues for all the rides. The worst thing is the café – it was very busy and there wasn't a table for us. The tickets are also quite expensive at the weekend.

It was a good day and I want to visit again. But next time, I'm going to buy tickets on a Monday because the tickets are cheap and the theme park isn't crowded.

3 **Read the review again and answer the questions.**

1 Why was Roxy at *Stormworld*?
2 Which was her favourite ride?
3 What was the problem?
4 Is she going to go again?

4 **Look at the Useful language. How do you say these expressions in your language?**

Useful language

Positive and negative comments

There are a lot of good ... at ...
The best ... is ...
I think that's a good idea.
However, there are some problems.
The worst thing is the ...

5 **Read the Look! box. Copy and complete the sentences with your own ideas.**

Look! ***so***

We use *so* to explain the results of a situation.
It was my birthday last Saturday, ***so*** *I was at* Stormworld.
It was really crowded, ***so*** *there were long queues for all the rides.*

It's raining, so *I'm not going to play football.*
1 I'm hungry, so ...
2 It's Friday, so ...
3 Today is my birthday, so ...

6 **Write a review of a place you know. Follow the steps in the Writing plan.**

Writing plan

Prepare

› Choose a place you know (e.g. a theme park, a café, sports centre etc.)
› Make notes about:
  - When/Why you were there
  - The good things about the place
  - The bad things about the place
  - Are you going to visit again?

Write

› Write your review.
› Use the expressions from the **Useful language** box.
› Use *so* to explain results of situations.

Reflect

› Check your grammar: *be*: past simple and *be going to*.
› Check your spelling and punctuation.

W **Writing summary:** WB p.92
R **Review: Units 7–9** SB pp.104–105
P **Project: Units 7–9** SB pp.110–111
L **Literature: Units 7–9** SB pp.116–117
LS **Language summary: Unit 9** SB p.126

CONTENTS

REVIEW
UNITS 1–3

READING

1 **Read about Elena. Choose the correct words to complete the text.**

Two years in the UK

I'm Elena and I'm thirteen. I'm from [1] *Spain / Spanish*, but I live in Cambridge, in the UK with my family. My parents [2] *is / are* teachers and we're here for two years. I have [3] *a / an* brother called Toni. He [4] *'s / 're* eleven.

My school in Cambridge is good and the lessons are interesting. It's an international school and my classmates are from all over the world. My best friend is [5] *a / an* Argentinian girl called Martina. [6] *Her / His* desk is next [7] *to / of* my desk in our Science class.

There [8] *'s / are* lots of beautiful buildings in Cambridge, but there [9] *isn't / aren't* a beach! In Spain, our house is in front [10] *to / of* a beautiful beach. My cat is in Spain at my [11] *grandmas' / grandma's* house. I'm [12] *sad / happy* because it isn't here with me!

2 **Put the words in the correct order to make questions about Elena.**

1 Elena / British / is / ?
2 brother / her / how old / is / ?
3 from / best friend / is / where / her / ?
4 beach / there / in / a / Cambridge / is / ?
5 cat / Elena's / is / where / ?

3 **Answer the questions from Exercise 2.**

LISTENING

4 R1 **Listen to the descriptions of the houses. Match them to the people.**

1

Khloé Kardashian

a

2

John Legend and Chrissy Teigen

b

3

Jay Z and Beyoncé

c

5 R1 **Listen again. Are the sentences true (T) or false (F)?**

1 There are seven bedrooms in Khloé Kardashian's house.
2 There's a swimming pool in her garden and a cinema in her house.
3 There are ten bathrooms in John Legend and Chrissy Teigen's house.
4 They live in Justin Bieber's old house.
5 Jay Z and Beyoncé's house is in Los Angeles, in the USA.
6 Blue Ivy, Rumi and Sir are their children.

SPEAKING

6 **Work in pairs. Look at pictures A and B. Find ten differences.**

In picture A there's a computer on the desk, but in picture B there isn't a computer.

WRITING

7 **Look at a picture of Poppy and her family. Write sentences about the picture with the words in the box.**

brother	dad	laptop	light	mum	pet
phone	plant	sofa	table	window	

This is a picture of a living room. In this room, there's …

There are …

TEST YOUR MEMORY!

- How many adjectives can you say in twenty seconds?
- Name three countries and their nationalities.
- Name five things in your classroom.
- Name three people in your family and how they are related to you.
- Name four rooms in a house.
- Name five things your living room.
- Make a question for your partner with *be*.
- Say two things you *are* and two things you *aren't*.
- Say five things you can see. Use articles or plurals.
- Say five things you can see. Use possessive adjectives or *'s*.
- What can you see out of the window. Use *there is* / *there are*.
- Describe three things in your bedroom. Use prepositions of place.

REVIEW UNITS 4–6

READING

1 Read about Nils's life in Tromsø. Complete the text with the correct forms of the verbs in the box.

get up	go	have	like	not like	live
meet	not stay	play	visit	want	work

Life in Tromsø

My name's Nils and I'm Norwegian. I [1] … in Tromsø, a small city in the north of Norway. It's in the Arctic Circle and in the summer the sun doesn't go down – that means it's never dark! I [2] … the summer because it's fun. We usually [3] … dinner quite late, and I often [4] … my friends in the evening. We [5] … to the beach or we [6] … football in the park.

Everything is different in the winter and the days are very short. There is only light for three hours each day! It's dark outside, but we [7] … at home all day. We [8] … and go to school! My mum [9] … the winter because it's very dark, but she [10] … in a hotel and she's usually very busy. A lot of tourists [11] … Tromsø in the winter because they [12] … to see the Northern Lights – they're very beautiful!

2 Read the text again. Answer the questions.

1 When is it never dark in Tromsø?
2 Why does Nils like the summer?
3 Where does he go with his friends?
4 How many hours of light are there in the winter?
5 Where does Nils's mum work?
6 Why do tourists visit Tromsø?

LISTENING

3 R2 Listen to the dialogues. What food and drink do Lara and Jamie order?

4 R2 Listen again and answer the questions.

1 Who does Lara order food for?
2 Where is her table?
3 How much does her food cost?
4 When does Jamie drink coffee?
5 Why doesn't he want water?
6 How much does his drink cost?

5 R2 Choose the correct words to complete the sentences. Listen again and check.

1 **Server:** Hello. What *would* / *do* you like?
2 **Lara:** Hi, *I like* / *I'd like* a burger and chips, and a coffee, please.
3 **Server:** Do you like *a sandwich* / *sandwiches*?
4 **Jamie:** What drinks *do you have* / *have you*?
5 **Jamie:** I drink coffee in the morning, but I *don't* / *doesn't* drink it in the afternoon.

SPEAKING

6 Work in pairs. Use the question words and the pictures to ask and answer questions.

A: What time do you get up? *B: At quarter to eight.*

1

What time ...?

2

Where ...?

3

What ...?

4

How often ...?

5

When ...?

6

Where ...?

7

What ...?

8

How often ...?

WRITING

7 Think about your perfect weekend. Copy and complete the sentences and add your own ideas.

On my perfect weekend, I get up at nine o'clock. I never get up early ...

1 I get up at ...
2 I have ... for breakfast.
3 In the morning, I meet ...
4 We go to ...
5 For lunch, I have ...
6 In the afternoon, I ...

TEST YOUR MEMORY!

What do you usually have for breakfast?

Name three things you don't like to eat or drink.

What would you like to eat or drink now?

Say four things you do every day.

Name one thing you use, one thing you learn and one thing you want.

Think of something you never do.

Ask your partner a question with *How often ...?*

Name two things you can ride.

Write one question with *where* and one question with *why*.

Think of a place in your country you would like to visit.

Name three expressions of frequency.

Say an important date and why it is important.

REVIEW
UNITS 7–9

READING

1 Read Katie's email to a friend. Complete the text with the words in the box.

are	boat	can	can't	going	having
hotel	I'm	is	taxi	there	were

Hi Alfie!

I'm on holiday with my family in the city of Cartagena in Colombia. Right now, we're in a beautiful square called Plaza Bolivar. Check out this picture!

We're [1] … lunch and watching people – it's really crowded and noisy. Some children [2] … playing football, a man [3] … singing and a woman is selling clothes. After lunch, we're going to travel by [4] … to a place called Las Bovedas. There are some cool shops and [5] … going to buy a new bag.

We [6] … at a chocolate museum yesterday. [7] … were classes on how to cook with chocolate. Now I [8] … make delicious hot chocolate!

Tomorrow I'm going to go surfing. I'm really excited! My brother isn't [9] … to come with us because he [10] … swim. Then, we're going to travel to an island called Tierra Bomba. We're going to get a bus from our [11] … and then there's a [12] … to the island.

Katie

2 Correct the sentences in your notebooks.

1. Katie is on holiday with her friends.
2. She's having breakfast in Plaza Bolivar.
3. A woman is singing and a man is selling clothes.
4. Katie's mum is going to buy a new bag.
5. Katie was at a chocolate museum last week.
6. Her brother is going to go surfing tomorrow.

LISTENING

3 R3 Felix wants to play tennis. Listen to three dialogues. Who is he going to play tennis with?

4 R3 Listen again. Copy and complete the table with the places the people are and the activities they are doing now.

Person	Place	Activity
 Anna		
 Stan		
 Emma		

5 R3 Copy and complete the sentences from the audio with the correct forms of the verbs in brackets. Listen again and check.

1. What … you … at the moment? (do / present continuous)
2. I … tennis tomorrow. (play / *be going to*)
3. I … my cousins tomorrow. (visit / *be going to*)
4. I … ! (not swim / present continuous)
5. My little brother … his swimming lesson. (have / present continuous)
6. I … at the swimming pool yesterday. (be / past simple)
7. … you … tennis, Emma? (play / *can*)
8. We … there all morning. (not be / *be going to*)

SPEAKING

6 Work in pairs. Ask and answer the questions.

1 How often do you go to the library?

2 Do you prefer to travel by bus or by train? Why?

3 What's the weather like today?

4 What are you going to buy next time you go to a shop?

5 Where do you go when it's raining?

6 Which sports can you play well?

7 When was the last time you were in the mountains?

8 What are you going to do next time you go to the beach?

WRITING

7 You're going to visit Harristown next weekend. Read the tourist information leaflet and the weather report. Write about your weekend plans.

On Friday, I'm not going to go to the beach because it's going to be cold. I'm going to ...

THINGS TO DO IN HARRISTOWN

Harris Beach
Two boat trips every day at 10 a.m. and 2 p.m. Tickets: £15

White Mountains
Skiing day trip 9 a.m. – 6 p.m. Tickets: £150

The Franklin Art Museum
Open 10 a.m. – 5 p.m. Tickets: £8 (adults), £6 (under 16s)

Westwood Forest
Ride a mountain bike! £4 per hour / £10 per day

City Bus Tour
See the whole city on a two-hour bus tour. Every hour from 9.30 a.m. – 4.30 p.m. Tickets: £10

WEATHER REPORT

Friday	Saturday	Sunday
1°	12°	20°

TEST YOUR MEMORY!

- Say as many sports as you can in 30 seconds.
- Say two things you can do and two things you can't do.
- Name four useful skills.
- Say one thing you love and one thing you hate.
- Think of a town you know and make a list of places in it.
- Describe a place you know. Use adjectives to describe it.
- Say what someone you know is doing now.
- Write two questions in the present continuous.
- Make a list of the places you were in last week.
- Describe the typical weather in your country in December.
- Name five types of transport.
- Write two sentences about your future plans.

PROJECT UNITS 1–3

TASK

Create a poster about your life

I can plan and make a poster.

PREPARE

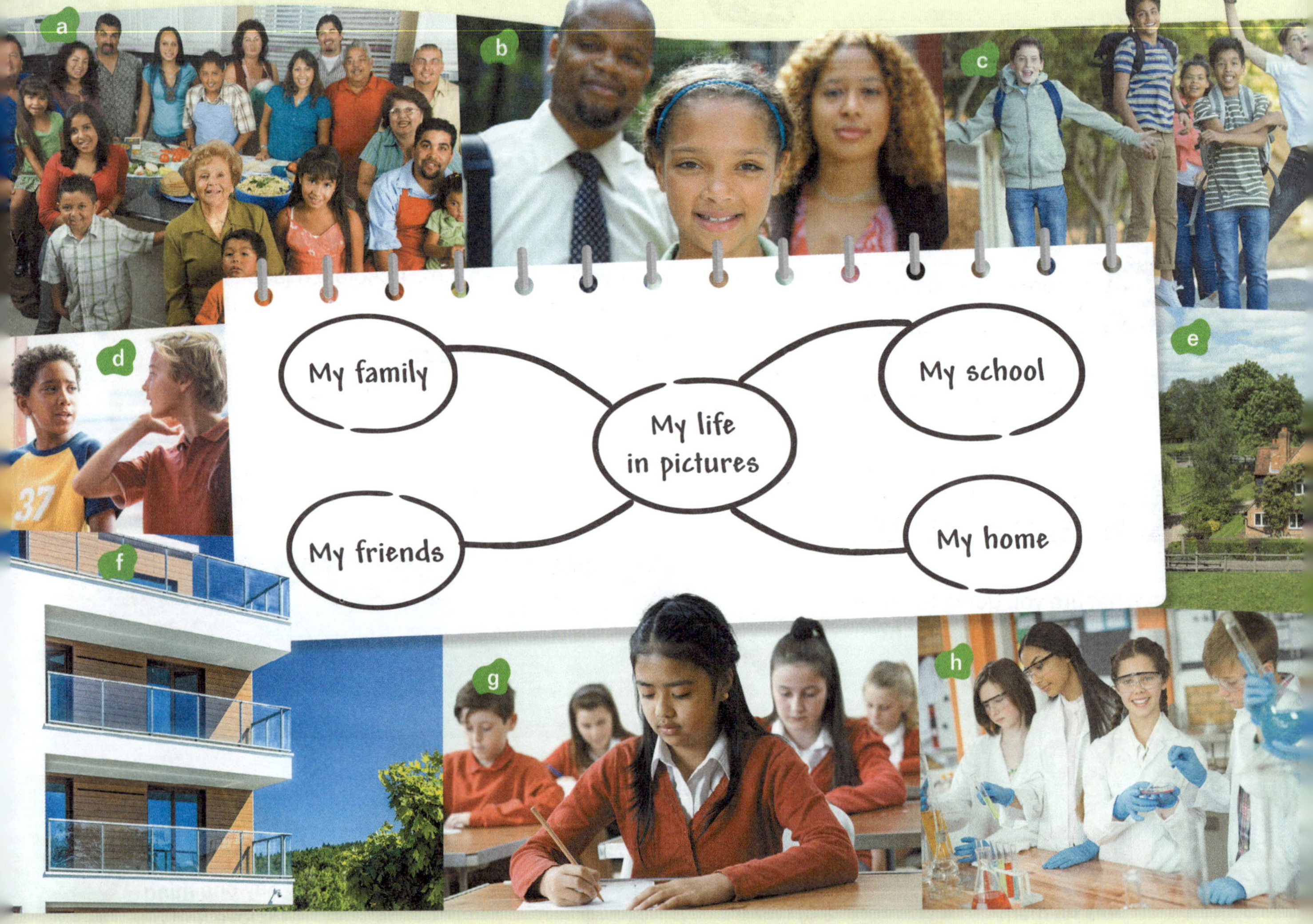

Step 1 **Get ideas**

› Match the photos with the categories in the mind-map.

› Tell your partner which photos are similar to your family, friends, home and school.

My family is the same as this family. My family is big!

Step 2 **Choose pictures**

› Draw pictures or find photos about you for the four categories.

› Choose the best picture for each category.

21st Century skills **Think critically**

Think about which pictures are interesting for other people. How do the pictures make other people feel?

Step 3 **Do your research**

› Work in pairs. Tell your partner which pictures you want to include in your poster. Do they agree?

Look! **Feedback**

Get feedback by asking for other people's opinions. Do their ideas help you with your work?

DO

Step 4 **Plan your poster**

- Decide if your poster is on paper or on a computer.
- Make a sketch of your poster. Decide where each picture goes.

Step 5 **Write the text for your poster**

- Write the text to explain the pictures on your poster. Use the **Useful language** box to help you.
- Give your text to another student to check your spelling and punctuation.

Step 6 **Create your poster**

- Print or draw your poster.
- Add the text to explain the pictures.
- Display your poster for your class to see.

REFLECT

Step 7 **Evaluate the posters**

- Look at all the posters and ask questions.
  How old are your brothers?
  Is this your teacher?
- Choose the posters you like. Why are the pictures interesting?

Step 8 **Reflect**

- Think about your poster. Is there anything you can improve on your poster?

Useful language

This is my home/school/family.
... is my best friend/cousin.
He/She/It is(n't) ...
These are my friends/brothers/sisters.
They are(n't) ...
There are ... bedrooms. My bedroom is ...
There are ... at our school, but there aren't any ...

My life in pictures

My family

This is my family on a special day – it's my dog's first birthday! His name's Bailey. My mum and dad and my two big brothers are in the photo, too.

My friends

These are my friends at a Halloween party. The boy with the green face is Eric – he's funny! The girl behind Eric is Esther. She's my best friend.

My school

This is a Drama class at our school. Drama classes are on Monday and Friday and they're fun! It's my favourite subject. The other classes at school are boring!

My house

Our house is small, but our garden is big. There aren't any interesting photos of my house, but this is my tree house! It's in our garden and it's very cool. There are posters on the walls and there's an old sofa for me and my friends!

PROJECT UNITS 4-6

TASK

Do a survey about your classmates

I can do a survey and present the results.

PREPARE

a

b

c

d

Music

1 **What musical instrument do you play?**
guitar | violin | piano | other | no instrument

2 **Where do you listen to music?**
at home | outside | at school | a different place

Food and drink

3 **What meals do you cook?**
breakfast | lunch | dinner | all meals | I don't cook

4 **What's your favourite food?**
pizza | burger and chips | pasta | salad | other

e

f

Going out

5 **How often do you visit museums?**
every weekend | once a month | once or twice a year | never

6 **Where do you go with your friends?**
the beach | the cinema | the park | other

g

h

Home life

7 **What do you do in the evening?**
watch TV | play videogames | chat with friends | read | other

8 **Where do you do your homework?**
at home | at school | on the bus | other

Step 1 Get ideas

- Match the pictures with the questions on the notepad.
- Work in pairs. Ask and answer the questions. Do you have the same answers?

Step 2 Prepare your survey

- Work in groups of four. Which topic is most interesting for you?
- Talk with other groups. Decide on one topic for each group.
- Write four questions about this topic to ask in your survey.
- Think of options as answers for people to choose from.

Look! Collaboration

Sometimes, two groups want to choose the same topic. Work together as a class to make sure you cover each topic.

Step 3 Do your survey

- Each person in the group asks one question to everyone in the class.
- Record the results in your notebook.
- Join your group and share your results.

DO

Step 4 Present your results.

- Talk about how to present the results of your survey.
- Decide if you want to present your tables or charts on a computer or on paper.
- Make tables and charts to show your results.

21st Century skills Get creative

What are the different ways to show the results of your survey? Do you know any fun or interesting ways? Think about pictures and emojis, etc.

Step 5 Prepare to speak

- Each person in the group talks about the results of one question.
- Make notes about what you want to say. Use the **Useful language** box to help you.
- Practise your presentation in a group.

Step 6 Present your survey

- Display your tables and charts for the rest of the class to see.
- As a group, present the results.

REFLECT

Step 7 Evaluate the projects

- Listen to the other presentations. Which is your favourite?
- Say which results are interesting or important. Why?

Step 8 Reflect

- Think about your presentation. Is there anything you can improve?

Useful language

The question is, ...
This chart/table shows ...
Five people like ...
Everybody likes ...
Most people (don't) play ...
Nobody listens to ...
... people do other things, such as ...

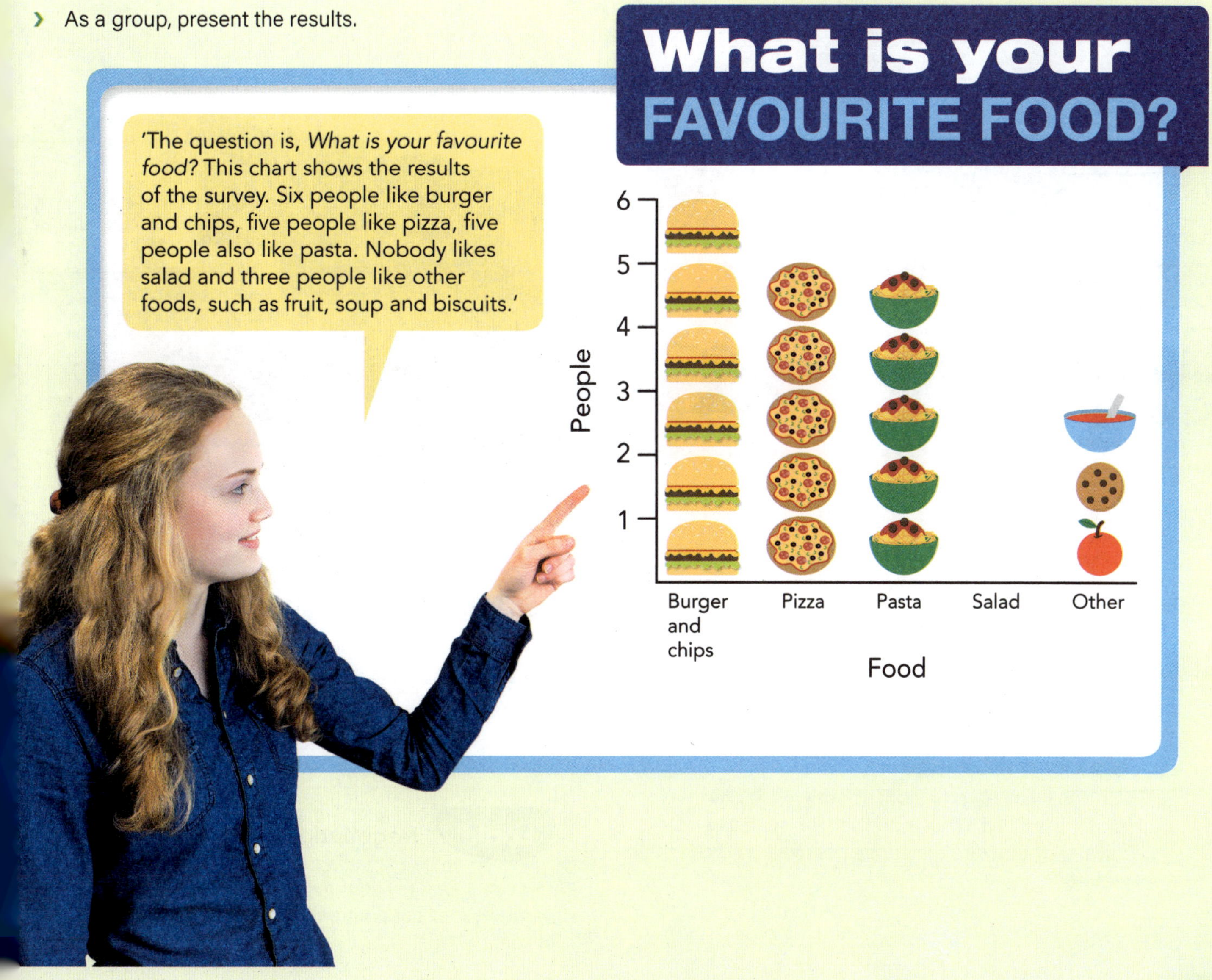

PROJECT
UNITS 7–9

TASK

Design your own island

I can collaborate to design an island.

PREPARE

Step 1 **Get ideas**

› Look at the pictures of life on an island. Copy and complete the table with examples from the pictures.

Nature	Transport	Activities	Places
sea			

21st Century skills Find out

Use the internet to find out about private islands. Where are they? What is on them? How do people travel to them? Are they similar or different from the pictures?

Step 2 **Categorize your ideas**

› Write a list of things you <u>need</u> on your island and a list of things you <u>would like</u> on your island.

Need: houses for people

Would like: a swimming pool

› Work in pairs. Compare your lists and decide what things you are going to have on your island.

› Complete a table like in Step 1 with the things you are going to have on your island.

Look! **Negotiation**

You can't use only your own ideas. Listen to your partner's ideas and agree on a list that is OK for both of you.

DO

Step 3 Design your island

- Decide if you want to design your poster on a computer or on paper.
- Draw your island with all of the features you agreed on.
- Print out or download photos to use in your poster.

Step 4 Write the text for your poster

- Write the text to explain all the features on your island. Use the **Useful language** box to help you.
- Give your text to another pair to check spelling and punctuation.

Step 5 Create your poster

- Arrange the drawing and the text on the poster.
- Display your poster for the class to see.

REFLECT

Step 6 Evaluate the projects

- Look at your classmates' islands.
- Which islands do you like? What's your favourite thing about the islands?

Step 7 Reflect

- Think about your own project. Is there anything you can improve on your poster?

Useful language

These people are ... on the beach / in the sea.
It's a beautiful/quiet/nice place.
The ... is very quiet/crowded.
You can/can't ... on the island.
We're going to (build) ... on the island.
There was/were ... but now there's / there are ...

LITERATURE
UNITS 1–3

BEFORE YOU READ

1 **Work in pairs. Imagine you're a new student at a school. Choose the best option to complete the sentences for the activities in the box.**

I think it's easy to ...
I think it's difficult to ...

find classrooms	join clubs	make new friends
talk to teachers	understand lessons	

2 **Read the outline to *A surprise for Emma*. Complete the sentences with the correct words.**

1 Emma is the *new / old* student in the class.
2 It's *easy / difficult* for Emma to make new friends.
3 She's quiet with other people because she's *noisy / shy.*
4 She is usually *at home / with friends* at the weekend.

OUTLINE

A surprise for Emma

Emma Crace is twelve years old. She lives with her parents and her little brother. She's the new student in her school and she doesn't have any friends yet. It isn't easy for Emma to make friends – she's quiet around other people because she's shy. The other students are noisy and they go out together at the weekend and have fun. Emma stays at home. She's usually in her bedroom with her pet parrot, Rolo.

READ

3 L1 **Read and listen to Part one of the story. Look at the picture. Find the people and things in the box.**

a cage	Emma	Kevin	Rolo

'Congratulations, everyone – it's Friday! What are your plans for the weekend?'

Ms Booth stands in front of the board and speaks to the students. Emma sits at the back of the classroom. There is nobody next to her.

'The beach!' says one student.

'It's Caitlin's birthday party tomorrow,' says another student. 'It's at the beach.'

'Lovely,' says Ms Booth. 'Emma, are you going to Caitlin's party?'

The other children turn and look at Emma.

'Um ...,' her face is red because she's embarrassed. 'No, I'm not.'

'OK,' says Ms Booth. 'Maybe something with your family, then?'

'Um ..., I don't know,' says Emma. She feels very shy.

'Ha!' a boy laughs. His name is Toby. Emma doesn't like him.

'Be quiet, Toby!' shouts Ms Booth. She's angry with Toby. 'Have a good weekend, Emma.'

She's a nice teacher, thinks Emma.

It's Saturday morning and Emma is in her bedroom. There's a cage next to the bed. Emma's pet parrot, Rolo, is in the cage.

'Oh Rolo, I'm very bored today,' Emma says.

There's a voice behind her bedroom door. 'Emma?' It's Kevin, her little brother.

'What do you want?' she asks.

'Is there someone in your room with you?'

Emma says nothing.

'Ha! You're talking to Rolo again!' he laughs.

'Go away!' says Emma, and she looks at the cage.

'I want to go to the beach with the others, but I'm scared,' she says.

'Don't be scared.'

Emma is very surprised. 'Who said that?' Is Kevin behind her door again?

Rolo looks at her. 'Don't be scared, Emma.'

'Aagh!' Emma jumps. 'Rolo? Is that you?'

'Yes, it's me.'

'But … you're talking!'

'I know I'm talking! Now come here. I have an idea.'

Emma puts her head close to the cage and listens.

4 Word Power Read the story again. Find the adjectives in the box. Match the adjectives with the pictures.

angry	embarrassed	scared	surprised

5 Read the story again. Are the sentences true (T) or false (F)?

1 Emma sits next to her friends in the classroom.
2 Toby is her friend.
3 Ms Booth is a nice teacher.
4 Emma's classmates go to the beach on Saturday.
5 Emma goes to the beach on Saturday.
6 Emma is in her bedroom with another person.
7 Emma is very happy.
8 Her parrot talks to her.

6 L2 Work in pairs. Choose what you think Rolo says? Listen and check.

Rolo wants to …

a stay in the cage
b go outside
c eat breakfast

REFLECT

7 Work in pairs. Answer the questions.

1 Are you shy?
2 Do you know a shy person?
3 What is it difficult for shy people to do?

8 FIND OUT African Grey parrots are good at talking. Find out how many words they can learn.

Glossary

laugh the sound you make when you're happy or you think something is funny
cage a box with bars to keep animals or birds in
voice the sound you make when you speak or sing
idea a plan or suggestion

LITERATURE
UNITS 4-6

BEFORE YOU READ

1 **Work in pairs. What do you remember about Part one of the story, *A surprise for Emma*?**

2 **Read the outline to *A picnic in the park*. Complete it with the words in the box.**

beach	cage	friends
new	parrot	scared

OUTLINE

A picnic in the park

Emma is the [1] ... student in the class and she doesn't have any [2] ... . All of Emma's classmates go to a birthday party at the [3] ... . Emma wants to go to the party, but she is [4] ..., so she stays at home with her pet [5] ..., Rolo. Rolo talks to Emma. He wants Emma to open the [6] ... so they can go outside together.

READ

3 L3 **Read and listen to Part two of the story. Do Emma and Rolo have a good time?**

4 **Read the story again and answer the questions.**

1 Why is Rolo happy?
2 What does Rolo do in the kitchen?
3 Who gets to the park first?
4 What does Emma eat for the first time?
5 How often does Emma go to the park?
6 Where does Rolo see a big problem?

5 **Word Power** **Find verbs 1–4 in the story. Match them to their opposites a–d.**

1 arrive	b close
2 win	c start
3 open	a lose
4 stop	d leave

A picnic in the park

Emma opens the cage and Rolo steps out. He looks happy and he starts to fly around the bedroom.

'This is fun!' he shouts.

Emma laughs. 'You're so happy!'

'I'm happy because I'm not in a cage,' says Rolo.

'I know what you mean,' says Emma. 'I sometimes feel like I'm in a cage, too.'

'But we aren't in a cage now. We're free!' says Rolo. 'Let's go outside.'

They go downstairs together. Rolo flies into the kitchen and puts some snacks in a bag. 'Now, take the bag and let's go,' he says.

They leave the house. Emma walks slowly with her head down. She feels shy.

'Emma, look at me!' says Rolo. 'Let's run to that park!

'Run? I never run,' she says. 'I'm not good at running.

'Come on!' says Rolo and he flies past her.

'Wait!' Emma doesn't want to run, but she does. She feels good and she starts to laugh. 'Rolo … this is fun!' she shouts.

Emma arrives at the park first. 'I win!' she says.

They sit down under a tree. Rolo opens the bag. 'Would you like some nuts?'

'Um ... no, thanks. I always have crisps for my snack.'

'What? Do you eat the same things every day? That's boring!' They both laugh. 'Come on ... have some.'

Emma eats some nuts. 'Mmm … they're delicious!' she says. She looks around and smiles. 'This is a nice park. I walk past it every day, but I never go in.'

'It's beautiful!' says Rolo and he flies up. 'It's a beautiful park … it's a beautiful city.' He flies higher and higher. 'It's a beautiful world!' he shouts. 'Hey, Emma, I can see the sea! I can see the beach!'

Emma watches him and laughs. Then suddenly, Rolo stops and shouts, 'Oh no!' He flies down to Emma.

'Rolo, what's wrong?'

'Emma, there's a big problem at the beach.'

6 L4 **Work in pairs. Look at the pictures. What do you think Rolo sees at the beach? Listen and check.**

1

2

3

REFLECT

7 **THINK CRITICALLY** **Work in groups. Choose the best answer for the questions.**

1 Why does Emma say she feels like she's in a cage?
   - a Because her bedroom is small.
   - b Because she's scared and shy.
   - c Because there are lots of rules at school.

2 Why is Emma happy in the park?
   - a Because she wins the race with Rolo.
   - b Because she likes the snacks.
   - c Because she tries new things.

3 What do you think happens next?
   - a Emma goes to the beach with Rolo.
   - b Emma stays in the park.
   - c Emma and Rolo call the police.

Glossary

step out to leave a place, by moving away from it
fly move through the air like a bird or aeroplane
feel like to want to do something at a particular moment
shout to speak with a loud voice

LITERATURE
UNITS 7–9

BEFORE YOU READ

1 Work in pairs. Discuss the questions with a partner. Read the outline to Part three of the story and check your answers.

1 Is Emma happy at school? Why/Why not?
2 What is unusual about Rolo?
3 Where do Emma and Rolo have a picnic?
4 Where are Emma's classmates?
5 What dangerous thing does Rolo see?

OUTLINE

Emma saves the day!

Emma is a new student and she doesn't have friends at school because she's very shy. Her only friend is Rolo, her pet parrot. But Rolo is a special parrot – he can talk! Emma's classmates are at a birthday party at the beach, but Emma is in her room with Rolo. He asks Emma to let him out of the cage and together they go to the park for a picnic. They have fun and Emma feels happy. But then Rolo flies high up in the sky and sees that a big wave is coming towards the beach.

2 Work in pairs. Look at the picture. What are the people are doing?

Emma's shouting …

READ

3 L5 Read and listen to Part three of the story. Are all the children safe at the end of the story?

4 Read the story again. Copy and complete the sentences with the correct names.

1 … is reading a book.
2 … tells Emma the wave is close.
3 … counts the students.
4 … saves Toby's life.
5 … says sorry to Emma.
6 … offers Emma some cake.

Emma saves the day!

Emma runs with Rolo to the beach and they look around. Caitlin is playing tennis with a friend. Some people are dancing and the others are swimming or surfing. Ms Booth is sitting on the beach. She's reading a book.

Emma thinks, *I need to tell everyone about the wave, but I'm scared.* She closes her eyes.

Rolo says, 'Come on, Emma! You can do this!'

Emma runs to the other children. 'Listen, everyone!' she shouts. 'You need to leave the beach, now!'

The other students look at Emma. They're surprised and confused, but they don't leave the beach.

'How far is the wave from the beach?' Emma asks Rolo.

'It's very close,' says Rolo. 'It's going to be here in three minutes!'

Ms Booth stands up. 'Emma. Is this a joke?'

'No, Ms Booth. I'm serious,' Emma says. 'There's a big wave.'

'How big is this wave?' asks Ms Booth.

'It's enormous!'

Ms Booth sees the wave. She turns to the children and shouts. 'Everyone! Come here now!' The children are surprised, but they listen to their teacher.

'Wait. How many children are here?' She counts the students. 'There's one person missing!'

'It's Toby!' shouts Emma. Toby is swimming far from the beach and he can't hear Ms Booth.

Emma runs towards the sea. 'Stop!' shouts Ms Booth. But Emma doesn't stop. She's a good swimmer. She reaches Toby and they swim back to the beach.

Everyone runs to a hill above the beach. They watch the wave hit the beach. It covers everything with water and then goes out to sea again. Everyone looks at Emma.

'You saved my life, Emma,' says Toby. He looks embarrassed. 'I'm sorry I laughed at you.'

'That's OK,' she says.

'That was amazing, Emma,' says Caitlin. 'Thank you!'

Emma smiles at her. 'You're welcome … and happy birthday!' They both laugh.

'Would you like to have some birthday cake with us?' asks Caitlin.

'Yes, please,' says Emma, 'but first I need to talk to a friend.'

5 Word Power Complete the questions with the question words in the box. Check your answers in the text.

How big	How far	How many

1 ... is the wave from the beach?
2 ... is this wave?
3 ... children are here?

6 Work in pairs. Ask and answer the questions.

1 How many brothers and sisters do you have?
2 How far is your house from school?
3 How big is your bedroom?

7 L6 Listen to the next part of the story. Choose the correct answers.

1 Emma sits on the hill with *Ms Booth / Rolo*.
2 The children return to the *beach / school*.
3 Rolo *loves / hates* his cage.
4 Rolo wants to *stay in his cage / be free*.
5 Rolo is going to visit Emma every *day / week*.

REFLECT

8 GET CREATIVE Work in pairs. Make a book cover for the story about Emma and Rolo.

1 Think of a title for the story.
2 Draw a picture for the front cover.
3 Write a sentence to say what the story is about.

Glossary

surfing the sport of riding on a wave on a special board
wave a line of water moving across the sea
confused when you cannot think clearly
enormous extremely large
missing lost, or not in the right or usual place

LANGUAGE SUMMARY
UNIT 1

GRAMMAR

Articles

an	We use *an* before singular nouns that begin with vowels (*a, e, i, o, u*). **an** animal, **an** egg, **an** umbrella
a	We use *a* before singular nouns that begin with consonants (e.g. *b, c, d*, etc.). **a** window, **a** chair, **a** teacher

Plural nouns

Spelling rules	Singular	Plural
For most nouns: we add *-s*.	a chair an egg	chair**s** egg**s**
For nouns ending in *-ch, -s, -sh, -x* or *-z*: we add *-es*.	a box a watch	box**es** watch**es**
For nouns ending in *-f* or *-fe*: we remove *-f* or *-fe* and add *-ves*.	a shelf a knife	shel**ves** kni**ves**
For nouns ending in consonant + *-y*: we remove *-y* and add *-ies*.	a dictionary a story	dictionar**ies** stor**ies**
Irregular nouns	a woman a man a person a child	**women** **men** **people** **children**

be: affirmative and negative

	Affirmative	Negative
I	I**'m** a boy.	I**'m not** a girl.
you	You**'re** Mexican.	You **aren't** Spanish.
he	He**'s** in this class.	He **isn't** in Class 2.
she	She**'s** short.	She **isn't** tall.
it	It**'s** cheap	It **isn't** expensive.
we	We**'re** at school.	We **aren't** at home.
they	They**'re** red.	They **aren't** blue.

Rules

We use the verb *be* to give information about things and people.

After subject pronouns we usually use the short form.

*I **am** a teacher. = I**'m** a teacher.*

*She **is not** in class. = She **isn't** in class.*

*They **are** from Brazil = They**'re** from Brazil.*

VOCABULARY

Classroom objects

board
chair
computer
desk
door
headphones
laptop
pen
pencil
pencil case
rubber
ruler
shelf
smartphone
tablet
window

Adjectives

beautiful
big
boring
cheap
difficult
easy
expensive
happy
interesting
old
sad
short
small
tall
ugly
young

SPEAKING

Talking about days

What day is it today?
It's Monday/Tuesday, etc.
What day is the Maths lesson?
It's on Wednesday/Thursday, etc.

Talking about times

What time is it?
It's ten o'clock / quarter past nine, etc.
What time is the English lesson?
It's at half past three / quarter to twelve, etc.

WRITING

You and your school

I'm in Year ...
I'm a student at ...
It's a big/small/old/new school.
There are ... students.
My favourite day/subject is ...
I'm (not) in the school ... team.

Capital letters

We use capital letters:

- at the start of sentences: ***S**he's a girl.*
- with the subject pronoun, *I*: ***I**'m happy.*
- with names of people and places: ***A**lex is in **N**ew **Y**ork.*
- with countries and nationalities: *Sara is from **M**exico. She's **M**exican.*
- with days of the week: *Today is **M**onday.*

LANGUAGE SUMMARY
UNIT 2

GRAMMAR

Possessive adjectives

Subject pronoun	Possessive adjective	
I	**my**	I'm twelve and **my** sister is ten.
you	**your**	You're in Class 3. This is **your** teacher.
he	**his**	He's happy because **his** friends are here.
she	**her**	She's a student. **Her** uniform is blue.
it	**its**	It's a good shop. **Its** clothes are cheap.
we	**our**	We're from Spain. **Our** house is in León.
they	**their**	They're actors. **Their** jobs are cool.

Rules

We use possessive adjectives before nouns to show that something belongs to someone.

We use the same possessive adjectives for singular and plural nouns:

*This is **your** pen. These are **your** pens.*

Possessive *'s*

For names and singular nouns: we add ***'s***.	This is Marco**'s** desk. My teacher**'s** bag is red.
For plural nouns ending in *-s*: we add *'*	My parents' room is big. The classrooms' walls are white.
For irregular plural nouns: we add ***'s***.	The children**'s** toys are expensive. That's the men**'s** bathroom.

be: questions and short answers

	Questions	Short answers
I	**Am** I right?	Yes, I **am**. / No, I**'m not**.
you	**Are** you British?	Yes, you **are**. / No, you **aren't**.
he	**Is** he at home?	Yes, he **is**. / No, he **isn't**.
she	**Is** she happy?	Yes, she **is**. / No, she **isn't**.
it	**Is** it your pet?	Yes, it **is**. / No, it **isn't**.
we	**Are** we late?	Yes, we **are**. / No, we **aren't**.
they	**Are** they your cousins?	Yes, they **are**. / No, they **aren't**.

Rules

In questions the verb *be* comes before the subject.

Are you from Mexico? NOT ~~*You are from Mexico?*~~

In affirmative short answers we don't use the short from:

Yes, I am. NOT ~~*Yes, I'm.*~~

In negative short answers we usually use the short from:

*No, he **is not**. = No, he **isn't**.*

VOCABULARY

Family and pets

aunt
brother
cat
cousin
dad
dog
fish
grandma
grandpa
mum
parrot
rabbit
sister
uncle

Countries and nationalities

Argentina
Argentinian
Brazil
Brazilian
China
Chinese
Mexico
Mexican
Spain
Spanish
the UK
British
the USA
American
Turkey
Turkish

SPEAKING

Introductions

Hi/Hello.
I'm ... / My name's ...
Nice to meet you (too).

Asking for personal details

What's your name?
Where are you from?
How do you spell that?
How old are you?

WRITING

Describing personal photos

This is a photo of my family / our pet.
These are my parents / my friends.
This is my mother / our house.

and/but

We use *and* to add information:

*Juan is twelve years old **and** he's Spanish.*

We use *but* to contrast information:

*I'm British, **but** my best friend is Turkish.*

LANGUAGE SUMMARY

UNIT 3

GRAMMAR

There is / There are: affirmative and negative

	Affirmative	Negative
Singular	**There's an** apple in my bag.	**There isn't a** window in this room.
Plural	**There are some** pens on the desk.	**There aren't any** posters on the wall.

Rules

We usually use the short form of *there is* = *there's*.

We use *there's* / *there isn't* + *a*/*an* with singular nouns.

We use *there are* + *some* with plural nouns.

We use *there aren't* + *any* with plural nouns.

There is / There are: questions and short answers

	Questions	Short answers
Singular	**Is there a** balcony?	Yes, **there is**. / No, **there isn't**.
Plural	**Are there any** chairs?	Yes, **there are**. / No, **there aren't**.

Rules

We use *is there* + *a*/*an* to ask about singular nouns.

We use *are there* + *any* to ask about plural nouns.

We don't use the short form in affirmative short answers:

Yes, there is. NOT ~~*Yes, there's*~~.

Prepositions of place

The ball is **above** the box.

The ball is **behind** the box.

The ball is **in** the box.

The ball is **in front of** the box.

The ball is **next to** the box.

The ball is **on** the box.

The ball is **under** the box.

VOCABULARY

Rooms

balcony
bathroom
bedroom
dining room
garage
garden
hall
kitchen
living room
study

Objects in the home

bed
bath
cooker
fridge
light
plant
poster
shower
sofa
table
toilet
wardrobe

SPEAKING

Greetings

Hi! / Hello!
Good morning/afternoon.
How are you? / How are things?
(I'm) fine / (I'm) good / Not bad, thanks.
Bye. / Goodbye. / Goodnight.
See you later/tomorrow/on Saturday.

WRITING

Describing family homes

My house/flat is in ...
In our house, there are ...
Our flat is on the first/second/third floor.
My bedroom is next to / above / in front of ...
In front of / behind / next to the house, there's a ...

Punctuation

- Full stops (.) go at the end of sentences: *My house is in the city.*
- Commas (,) separate items in a list: *There's a desk, a chair and a computer.*
- Question marks (?) go at the end of questions: *Where's your house?*
- Exclamation marks (!) show emotion: *Your bedroom is very big!*

LANGUAGE SUMMARY UNIT 4

GRAMMAR

like / don't like

Affirmative 🙂	Negative ☹️
I **like** meat.	I **don't like** coffee.
I **like** vegetables.	I **don't like** eggs.
Questions	**Short answers**
Do you **like** chicken?	Yes, I **do**. / No, I **don't**.

Rules

🙂 We use *I like* + nouns in affirmative sentences.

☹️ We use *I don't like* + nouns in negative sentences.

We use *Do you like …?* + nouns to ask questions.

We use *do* or *don't* in short answers.

Yes, I do. NOT ~~*Yes, I like.*~~

would like

Affirmative	Questions	Answers
I'd (I **would**) **like** an apple, please?	**Would** you **like** a pancake?	**Yes, please.**
I'd (I **would**) **like** some biscuits, please?	**Would** you **like** some tea?	**No, thanks.**

Rules

We use *I would like* … to ask for things.

We usually use the short form: *I'd like …*

We use *Would you like …?* to offer things.

We use *Yes, please* and *No, thanks* to reply to offers with *would like*.

like and *would like*

like	*would like*
I **like** chocolate. It's delicious.	**I'd like** some water. I'm thirsty.
Do you **like** fish?	**Would** you **like** a banana?
Yes, I **do**. / No, I **don't**.	**Yes, please.** / **No, thanks.**

Rules

We use *like* to talk about things we like or don't like in general.

We use *would like* to offer or ask for things.

VOCABULARY

Food and drink

apple
banana
butter
cake
carrot
cheese
chicken
chocolate
coffee
eggs
fish
ice cream
juice
meat
milk
orange
potato
tea
tomato
water

Meals

biscuits
bread
breakfast
burger
cereal
chips
crisps
dinner
lunch
nuts
omelette
pancakes
pasta
pizza
rice
salad
sandwich
snacks
soup
toast

SPEAKING

Ordering in a café

Server

How can I help you? / What would you like?

Anything to drink? / Anything else?

It comes with …

That's … altogether.

Customer

I'd like …, please. / Can I have …, please?

Does … come with …?

That's all, thanks. How much is that?

WRITING

Describing your diet

This is what I eat in a typical week.

Many people have …, but I have …

There is/isn't a school cafeteria.

I have a packed lunch / school dinners.

My favourite … is …

It's delicious/horrible/healthy/unhealthy/sweet.

and/or

We use *and* to say we have two things together:

*I'd like a burger **and** chips.*

We use *or* to say we have one of two options:

*I have milk **or** orange juice for breakfast.*

LANGUAGE SUMMARY
UNIT 5

GRAMMAR

Present simple: affirmative

Subject pronouns	Affirmative
I	I **have** a shower in the morning.
you	You **have** cereal for breakfast.
he	Jacob **gets up** at 7.00.
she	Carmen **studies** Music at school.
it	School **finishes** at 4.00.
we	We **leave** home at 8.30.
they	They **make** a snack in the afternoon.

Rules

In the present simple affirmative, the subject comes before the verb. For the third person singular (*he/she/it*), the verb ends in *-s*: *get* > *gets*.

When the verb ends in *-ch, -sh, -ss, -x* and *-o* we add *-es*: *go* > *goes*.

When the verb ends in consonant + *-y*, we change the *-y* to *-ies*: *study* > *studies*. The third person singular of *have* is *has*.

Present simple: negative

Subject pronouns	Negative
I	I **don't call** my friends on the phone.
you	You **don't drink** coffee for breakfast.
he	Juan **doesn't live** in Madrid.
she	Linda **doesn't travel** by bus.
it	My house **doesn't have** a garden.
we	We **don't wear** jeans at school.
they	They **don't work** in an office.

Rules

In the present simple negative, when the subject is *I, you, we* or *they*, we add *don't* before the verb to make it negative.

For the third person singular (*he, she, we* or *it*), we add *doesn't* before the verb to make it negative.

We use *don't/doesn't* + infinitive:

She doesn't teach French. NOT ~~*She doesn't teaches French*~~.

Present simple: questions and short answers

Questions	Short answers
Do you **study** French?	Yes, I **do**. / No, I **don't**.
Does Liam **play** the drums?	Yes, he **does**. / No, he **doesn't**.

Rules

We form questions with *do/does* + subject + the infinitive of the verb.

In affirmative short answers we use *do/does*.

In negative short answers we use *don't/doesn't*.

VOCABULARY

Daily routine

do (my) homework
finish school
get dressed
get home
get up
go to bed
have a shower
have breakfast (lunch/dinner)
leave home
make a snack
start school
study Maths (English, etc.)

Common verbs

call
drink
eat
know
live
meet
teach
travel
use
want
wear
work

SPEAKING

Suggesting

Would you like to ...?
Do you want to ...?
What about ...?
Let's ...
Why don't we ...?

Responding

That's a good/great idea!
That sounds good/great!
I think it's too expensive/cold/late.
Sorry, but I don't feel like it.
Maybe.

WRITING

Describing general habits

In the UK, most people/schools ...
Some people/schools ..., but others ...
Usually, ...
... at about 9.00/10.00.

because

We use *because* to explain the reason for an action:

I get up late on Sunday ***because*** *I don't have school.*
He makes a snack after school ***because*** *he's always hungry when he arrives at home.*

LANGUAGE SUMMARY
UNIT 6

GRAMMAR

Adverbs of frequency

100%	I'm **always** hungry after school.
	Sam **usually** watches TV on Saturday.
	We **sometimes** have fish for lunch.
0%	She's **never** late for English class.

Rules

We use adverbs of frequency to talk about how often we do things.

We put adverbs of frequency before most verbs.

We put adverbs of frequency after the verb *be*.

Expressions of frequency

every ...	I listen to music **every day**. Karen has piano classes **every week**.
once/twice/ three times a ...	We go on holiday **twice a year**. They go shopping **three times a month**.

Rules

Expressions of frequency usually come at the end of a sentence.

We can use *every* + *day/week/month/year*, etc.

once = one time, *twice* = two times.

Wh- questions

Question word	*do/does*	Subject	Infinitive
What	**do**	you	**want to** have for dinner?
When	**does**	school	**start**?
Where	**does**	Maria	**live**?
Why	**do**	people	**study** History?
Who	**do**	you	**meet** at the weekend?

Rules

We make questions with question words to ask for specific information.

We form questions with question word + *do/does* + subject + infinitive.

We use *what* to ask about things.

We use *when* to ask about times.

We use *where* to ask about places.

We use *why* to ask about reasons.

We use *who* to ask about people.

VOCABULARY

Free-time activities

go on holiday
go shopping
listen to music
listen to podcasts
play the piano
play videogames
read a book
read a magazine
visit a museum
visit friends
watch an online video
watch TV

Seasons

spring
summer
autumn
winter

Months

January
February
March
April
May
June
July
August
September
October
November
December

Dates

first, second, third, etc.

SPEAKING

Asking for information

What time does it start/finish?
How much are the tickets?
How much do/does ... cost?
Who can I contact about ...?
Is there a ...? / Are there any ...?

Giving information

It starts at ... / It finishes at ...
Tickets are ...
Sorry, but I don't have that information.
You need to speak to/contact/email ...

WRITING

Writing an email

Hi, ... / Dear ...
How are you? / I hope you're well.
I want to tell you about ...
Write soon!
Bye / Take care

too/also

We use *too* at the end of a sentence:
I play the guitar and I play the piano, ***too.***
We use *also* before the verb:
I play the guitar and I ***also*** *play the piano.*

LANGUAGE SUMMARY
UNIT 7

GRAMMAR

can: affirmative and negative

Affirmative	Negative
I **can** speak Spanish and English. She **can** ride a horse.	They **can't** swim. Lucas **can't** dance salsa.

Rules

We use *can/can't* + infinitive to talk about our abilities.

can/can't is the same for all subjects.

can: questions and short answers

Questions	Short answers
Can you **play** the guitar?	Yes, I **can**. / No, I **can't**.
Can they **speak** Spanish?	Yes, they **can**. / No, they **can't**.

Rules

In questions, *can* comes before the subject.

In short answers we use *can* or *can't*.

like/love/hate

😍 I **love** football.
🙂 Corina **likes** gymnastics.
☹️ My friends **don't like** athletics.
😡 He **hates** tennis.

Rules

We use (*don't*) *like*/*love*/*hate* to talk about the activities we enjoy or don't enjoy.

Object pronouns

Subject pronoun	Object pronoun	
I	**me**	My parents watch **me** play football.
you	**you**	Can I call **you** after class?
he	**him**	Joao Felix is my favourite player – I love **him**!
she	**her**	This song is by Dua Lipa. Do you like **her**?
it	**it**	I hate volleyball. I never play **it**.
we	**us**	Our teacher gives **us** homework every week.
they	**them**	Spiders are horrible. I hate **them**.

Rules

We use object pronouns after verbs to substitute nouns.

VOCABULARY

Abilities

cook
dance
draw
drive
play the drums
ride a bike
ride a horse
sing
speak French
swim

Sports

athletics
baseball
basketball
climbing
football
gymnastics
martial arts
mountain biking
running
skateboarding
skiing
tennis

SPEAKING

Shopping for sports clothes

Shop assistant

Can I help you?
They're over there.
The ... are here.
Which size/colour do you want?
I'm sorry. We don't have any.
It's / They're ten pounds.

Customer

Do you have any ...?
I'd like small/medium/large, please.
Do you have it/them in ...?
How much is it / are they?
I'll take it/them.

WRITING

Interests and abilities

My favourite sport is ...
I like/don't like/hate/love ...
I think ... is fun/boring.
I'm (not) good at ...
I can/can't ... well.
I'd like to try ...

Modifiers

Modifiers make adjectives stronger or weaker:
*Susan is **really/very** good at gymnastics.*
*She's **quite** good at basketball.*
*She's **not very** good at tennis.*

LANGUAGE SUMMARY
UNIT 8

GRAMMAR

Present continuous: affirmative and negative

	Affirmative	Negative
I	I**'m working**.	I**'m not working**.
you	You**'re making** lunch.	You **aren't making** lunch.
he	Luca**'s running**.	Luca **isn't running**.
she	Kim**'s studying**.	Kim **isn't studying**.
it	The game**'s starting**.	The game **isn't starting**.
we	We**'re getting up**.	We **aren't getting up**.
they	They**'re taking** the bus.	They **aren't taking** the bus.

Rules

We use the present continuous to talk about things that are happening now.

In the present continuous we use the verb *be* and the *-ing* form of the main verb.

When the verb ends in *-e*, we remove the *-e* and add *-ing*:
take > *taking*

When the verb ends in consonant-vowel-consonant, we double the final consonant and add *-ing*:
run > *running*

Present continuous: questions and short answers

	Questions	Short answers
I	**Am** I **dreaming**?	Yes, I **am**. / No, I**'m not**.
you	**Are** you **working** today?	Yes, you **are**. / No, you **aren't**.
he	**Is** Tom **playing** football?	Yes, he **is**. / No, he **isn't**.
she	**Is** Eva **wearing** a hat?	Yes, she **is**. / No, she **isn't**.
it	**Is** your phone **ringing**?	Yes, it **is**. / No, it **isn't**.
we	**Are** we **driving** to school?	Yes, we **are**. / No, we **aren't**.
they	**Are** they **swimming**?	Yes, they **are**. / No, they **aren't**.

Rules

In questions we put the verb *be* before the subject and the *-ing* form of the main verb after the subject.

In short answers we use the verb *be*.

In *Wh-* questions, we use question words before the subject with the present continuous.

*'**What** is Sally doing?' 'She's playing the guitar.'*

*'**Where** are you going?' 'I'm going to school.'*

VOCABULARY

Places in a town

bank
factory
farm
hospital
hotel
library
market
shop
sports centre
supermarket
swimming pool
train station

Adjectives to describe places

clean
crowded
dangerous
dirty
empty
horrible
new
nice
noisy
old
quiet
safe

SPEAKING

Asking for directions

Excuse me, ...
I'm looking for ...
Is there a ... near here?
Is it far?
Is it near here?
How do you get there?

Giving directions

(Then) you go straight on.
You turn right/left.
You go past the ...
It's in front of / next to ...

WRITING

Arranging to meet

Do you want to ...?
Where/When do you want to meet?
Let's meet at ... / Shall we meet at ...?
Can we meet at ... instead?
See you (there) at ...

right now / at the moment

We use *right now / at the moment* to talk about actions happening now:
*I'm having dinner **right now**.*
***Right now**, I'm watching TV.*
*He's reading a good book **at the moment**.*
***At the moment**, I'm studying French.*

LANGUAGE SUMMARY
UNIT 9

GRAMMAR

be: past simple (affirmative and negative)

Affirmative	Negative
I/He/She/It **was** in London.	I/He/She/It **wasn't** in Madrid.
We/You/They **were** happy.	We/You/They **weren't** sad.

Rules

We use *was* and *were* to talk about situations in the past. We usually use the short form in the negative: *was not* = *wasn't*, *were not* = *weren't*.

be: past simple (questions and short answers)

Questions	Short answers
Were you in class yesterday?	Yes, I **was**. / No, I **wasn't**.
Was your sister happy with the present?	Yes, she **was**. / No, she **wasn't**.
Were your grandparents teachers?	Yes, they **were**. / No, they **weren't**.

Rules

In questions we put *was/were* before the subject.

In short answers we use *was/were* or *wasn't/weren't*.

be going to: affirmative and negative

	Affirmative	Negative
I	I**'m going to ride** my bike.	I**'m not going to walk**.
you	You**'re going to love** it!	You **aren't going to hate** it.
he	He**'s going to visit** you.	He **isn't going to visit** me.
she	She**'s going to swim** later.	She **isn't going to play** tennis.
it	It**'s going to be** late.	It **isn't going to arrive** on time.
we	We**'re going to work** hard.	We **aren't going to relax**.
they	They**'re going to stay** in a tent.	They **aren't going to stay** in a hotel.

Rules

We use *be* + *going to* + infinitive to talk about plans in the future.

be going to: questions and short answers

Questions	Short answers
Are you **going to study** Maths.	Yes, I **am**. / No, I**'m not**.
Is she **going to be** happy?	Yes, she **is**. / No, she **isn't**.
Are we **going to arrive** early?	Yes, we **are**. / No, we **aren't**.

Rules

In questions we put the verb *be* before the subject.

In affirmative short answers we don't use the short form:

Yes, she is. NOT ~~*Yes, she's.*~~

VOCABULARY

Weather

It's cloudy.
It's cold.
It's hot.
It's raining.
It's snowing.
It's sunny.
It's warm.
It's windy.

Nature

beach
field
flower
forest
lake
mountain
sea
tree

Transport

bike
boat
bus
car
motorbike
plane
scooter
taxi
train
tram

SPEAKING

Buying a train ticket

Customer

I'd like a (child) ticket to ..., please.
A single/return ticket, please.
When is the next train to ...?
Where do I go?

Assistant

Do you want a single or a return?
The next train leaves at ...
The train leaves from platform ...

WRITING

Positive and negative comments

There are a lot of good ... at ...
The best ... is ...
I think that's a good idea.
However, there are some problems.
The worst thing is the ...

so

We use *so* to explain the results of a situation:
It's raining, ***so*** *we're going to take a taxi.*
I'm hungry, ***so*** *I'm going to make a snack.*

IRREGULAR VERBS LIST

Infinitive		Past simple		Past participle	
be	/biː/	was/were	/wəz, wɒz, wə(r), wɜː(r)/	been	/bɪn, biːn/
become	/bɪ'kʌm/	became	/bɪ'keɪm/	become	/bɪ'kʌm/
begin	/bɪ'gɪn/	began	/bɪ'gæn/	begun	/bɪ'gʌn/
break	/breɪk/	broke	/brəʊk/	broken	/'brəʊkən/
bring	/brɪŋ/	brought	/brɔːt/	brought	/brɔːt/
build	/bɪld/	built	/bɪlt/	built	/bɪlt/
buy	/baɪ/	bought	/bɔːt/	bought	/bɔːt/
can	/kən, kæn/	could	/kəd, kʊd/		
catch	/kætʃ/	caught	/kɔːt/	caught	/kɔːt/
choose	/tʃuːz/	chose	/tʃəʊz/	chosen	/'tʃəʊzn/
come	/kʌm/	came	/keɪm/	come	/kʌm/
cost	/kɒst/	cost	/kɒst/	cost	/kɒst/
do	/də, du/	did	/dɪd/	done	/dʌn/
draw	/drɔː/	drew	/druː/	drawn	/drɔːn/
drink	/drɪŋk/	drank	/dræŋk/	drunk	/drʌŋk/
drive	/draɪv/	drove	/drəʊv/	driven	/'drɪvn/
eat	/iːt/	ate	/eɪt, et/	eaten	/'iːtn/
fall	/fɔːl/	fell	/fel/	fallen	/'fɔːlən/
feel	/fiːl/	felt	/felt/	felt	/felt/
find	/faɪnd/	found	/faʊnd/	found	/faʊnd/
fly	/flaɪ/	flew	/fluː/	flown	/fləʊn/
get	/get/	got	/gɒt/	got	/gɒt/
give	/gɪv/	gave	/geɪv/	given	/'gɪvn/
go	/gəʊ/	went	/went/	gone/been	/gɒn, biːn/
have	/həv, hæv/	had	/hæd/	had	/hæd/
hear	/hɪə(r)/	heard	/hɜːd/	heard	/hɜːd/
know	/nəʊ/	knew	/njuː/	known	/nəʊn/
learn	/lɜːn/	learnt/learned	/lɜːnt, lɜːnd/	learnt/learned	/lɜːnt, lɜːnd/
leave	/liːv/	left	/left/	left	/left/
lose	/luːz/	lost	/lɒst/	lost	/lɒst/
make	/meɪk/	made	/meɪd/	made	/meɪd/
meet	/miːt/	met	/met/	met	/met/
read	/riːd/	read	/red/	read	/red/
run	/rʌn/	ran	/ræn/	run	/rʌn/
say	/seɪ/	said	/sed/	said	/sed/
see	/siː/	saw	/sɔː/	seen	/siːn/
sell	/sel/	sold	/səʊld/	sold	/səʊld/
send	/send/	sent	/sent/	sent	/sent/
sing	/sɪŋ/	sang	/sæŋ/	sung	/sʌŋ/
sit	/sɪt/	sat	/sæt/	sat	/sæt/
sleep	/sliːp/	slept	/slept/	slept	/slept/
speak	/spiːk/	spoke	/spəʊk/	spoken	/'spəʊkən/
stand	/stænd/	stood	/stʊd/	stood	/stʊd/
swim	/swɪm/	swam	/swæm/	swum	/swʌm/
take	/teɪk/	took	/tʊk/	taken	/'teɪkən/
teach	/tiːtʃ/	taught	/tɔːt/	taught	/tɔːt/
tell	/tel/	told	/təʊld/	told	/təʊld/
think	/θɪŋk/	thought	/θɔːt/	thought	/θɔːt/
throw	/θrəʊ/	threw	/θruː/	thrown	/θrəʊn/
wear	/weə(r)/	wore	/wɔː(r)/	worn	/wɔːn/
write	/raɪt/	wrote	/rəʊt/	written	/'rɪtn/

Richmond
58 St Aldates
Oxford
OX1 1ST
United Kingdom

ISBN: 978-84-668-2791-1
CP: 915776
© Richmond / Santillana Global S.L. 2021

All rights reserved. No part of this book may be reproduced, stored in a retrieval system or transmitted in any form by any means, electronic, mechanical, photocopying, recording or otherwise, without the prior permission in writing of the Publisher.

Publishing Director: Deborah Tricker

Publishers: Sue Ashcroft, Simone Foster

Content development: Sarah Almy, David Cole-Powney

Editor: Heidi Underwood

Proofreader: Jennifer Cottrill

Design Manager: Lorna Heaslip

Cover Design: Big Pink Fish

Design & Layout: emc design Ltd, Georgia Styring

Photo Research: Magdalena Mayo, Helen Kunzemann

Culture videos and vlogs: Digital Learning Associates

Vloggers: Chelsie Angeles, Erika Felton, Tally Kerr, Ruaridh Kidd, Jason Regal, Isa Sevilla, Maiku Wong

Audio Production: Tom Dick And Debbie Educational Media Productions

Grammar presentations and story animations, and *Keep moving!* digital board game: CCS Digital Education

We would like to thank Yolanda Muñoz Vivas for her valuable contribution to developing the material.

We would like to thank all those who have given their kind permission to reproduce material for this book:

Illustrators: Petros Bouloubasis c/o Advocate Art; Martyn Cain c/o Beehive Illustration; Simon Clare; The Boy Fitzhammond c/o NB Illustration; Guillaume Gennet c/o Lemonade Illustration Agency; Carl Harrison c/o Beehive Illustration; Ben Hasler c/o NB Illustration; Javier Joaquín c/o Beehive Illustration; Liz Kay c/o NB Illustration; Dusan Lakicevic c/o Beehive Illustration; Katie Mac c/o NB Illustration; Lilia Micelli c/o Advocate Art; Jason Pickersgill c/o NB Illustration; Andy Rowland c/o Advocate Art; Martin Sanders c/o Beehive Illustration; Mike Stonelake c/o NB Illustration; Stefano Tambellini c/o NB Illustration.

Photos: Images courtesy of Whole Earth Nature School; Iwan Baan; Kaiser Permanente Zion Medical Center; Kareem Waris @waspa_art; Badges and image reproduced by permission of Scouts (UK); ALAMY/ Pixel-shot, Joerg Boethling, EnVogue_Photo, True Images, Tim Gainey, Ojas Thosar, Richard Watkins, GSO Images, Arcaid Images, Mr Standfast, Paul Baldesare, CarolynClarke, Jeff Gilbert, Simon Dack, Hemis, WENN Rights Ltd, LANDMARK MEDIA, BenSchonewille; GETTY IMAGES SALES SPAIN/Julialine, njekaterina, Narongrit Sritana, Track5, Monkeybusinessimages, AJ_Watt. Compassionate Eye Foundation, MoMo, Westend61, Richard Clark, Massimiliano Clari, Creative Crop, Moorefam, Jordan Parks Photography, By IAISI, David Madison, bigtunaonline, Portra, Andersen Ross Photography Inc., Carol Yepes, Tifonimages, Thomas Winz, Yellow Dog Productions, Pagadesign, Jure Gasparic, Kai Oberhauser, Wittaya Bunjua, Michael Burrell, AYImages, Sean Gladwell, ET-ARTWORKS, Pearleye, KenDrysdale, Kevin Peterson, Adventtr, Sweetym, Tom Sibley, Peshkov, Natikka, Chictype, Popovaphoto, LdF, S-Cphoto, Surut Wattanamaetee, Littlewitz, Coprid, Cleristonribeiro, Klaus Vedfelt, Mel Yates, Nattawut Lakjit, Bernd Kelichhaus, Veerapong Boonporn, Hdere, Andrew Demie, 101cats, Kathrin Gabriel, Beautyoflife13, JGI/Jamie Grill, Gannet77, Rosemary Calvert, Dobrila Vignjevic, Nemke, Busa Photography, Robert Lewin, Zheka-Boss, ROMAOSLO, Shironosov, Image Source, No_limit_pictures, Richard Lewisohn, Kativ, STRDEL/AFP, WANDER WOMEN COLLECTIVE, Artparadigm, calvindexter, TennesseePhotographer, Blend Images – JGI/Jamie Grill, SDI Production, Nick David, Shannon Fagan, Theboone, Oliver Rossi, Morsa Images, Maskot, Stigur Mar Karlsson/Heimsmyndir, Geoff Manasse, Juliet White, Irina Babina, Glasshouse images, Nils Jacobi, Paskuk Lertbuaban, S-S-S, bluebright, johnwoodcock, Vesnaandjic, Thomas Barwick, Valeriy_G, SDI Productions, enjoynz, Fstop123, Copyright Crezalyn Nerona Uratsuji, aleksandarvelasevic, Poligrafistka, 221A, ELIKA, Gustave Munoz Soriano, Yurchello108, CiydemImages, Junghee Choi, SOPA Images, Emma McIntyre/ AMA2019. RoBeDeRo, VCG, Frank Hoensch, Leon Halip, Jon Kopaloff, Gulfimages, Sean Gallup, Beatriz Velasco, Samir Hussein, Colematt, Tetiana Lazunova, Ron Levine, Henrik Sorensen, Juanmonino, Priscilla Gragg, saemilee, bgblue, 4zevar, Alexxx1981, Roger Wright, Picture Alliance, Murdo MacLeod, Artrise, Cavan Images, AaronAmat, AngelaMedler, Fotosearch, Dwi Yulianto, Neilson Barnard, Presley Ann, Raymond Hall, Petri Oeschger, Alan Tunnicliffe, David-Prado, Malomy, Kali9, John P Kelly, supermimicry, Pawel Wewiorski, Andy Teo Aka Photocillin, WOJTEK RADWANSKI, Anadolu Agency, studio@iwan.com, Leni Schmidt, Mikroman6, Ronstik, Gary Ombler, Vladimirovic, Cenkerdem, Gerenme, Martin Deja, Oscar Wong, John Keeble, Benjamin Toth, Artem Perevozchikov, Sezer66, monticelllo, BsWei, Aaaniram, Louis Turner, Issarawat Tattong, Tatiana Mezhenina, Adriano La Naia, Richard Newstead, RichLegg, Georgeclerk, Omelchenko Andrii, Heritage Images, Jeff Overs, Kelvinjay, Jamie Casper, Nialif, Surong, RedHelga, Julichka, Piotr, Marcinski, Mbbirdy, Lucentius, PicturePartners, SvetlanaK, Mkistryn, JoeGough, Lauri Patterson, Unalozmen, Sumnersgraphicsinc, Okea, Coprid, Leeser87, JPecha, Hemant Mehta, Tim UR, Roman Samokhin, Smitt, KorobanovaMarina, Yoyochow23, PaulPaladin, Pineapple Studio, Johner Images, Letty17, Creative Crop, JoeGough, kenmind77, Kirin_photo, Skodonnell, Photocrea, Jenifoto, Kcline, Ryzhkov, Yalcinsonat1, Glowimages, Burazin, Comstock Images, ninochka, Arx0nt, Blackjake, Stefan Pogoreutschnig, Grace Cary, BURCU ATALAY TANKUT, Picture Alliance, Helin Loik-Tomson, Dontstop, Sergio Amiti, Shablon, SolStock, Darrin Klimek, Clubfoto, NightAndDayImages, Creative Crop, Narin Deniz Erkan, Mtreasure, Plej92, Yumehana, Semenovp, simon2579, Andresr, Vgajic, Axelle/Bauer-Griffin, Bruce Glikas, Steve Granitz, David M.Benett, Lorado, Agrobacter, Amy Sussman, Supersizer, Michael Gruber/Life Ball 2017, Steven Puetzer, MachineHeadz, Adamkaz, Yobro10, LindaYolanda & PeopleImages, John Giustina, Frank Rothe, Merrill Images, JupiterImages, Steve Mason, Nick David, Flying Colours Ltd, Portishead1, Mixetto, Ben Gingell, Diane Macdonald, Rayes, Peter M. Fisher, Daviles, BJI, LightFieldStudios, Tim Ockenden-PA Images, Gonzalo Azumendi, THEPALMER, JEWEL SAMAD, Gonzaol Azumendi, Halfpoint, 3sbworld, Patti Mundy, ShutterOK, Imagesbybarbara, SEAN GLADWELL, AmyLaughinghouse, Ian Gavan, Maria Jefferis, Joseph Okpako, Dougal Waters, Paul Morigi, Steve Granitz, Samir Hussein, FilippoBacci, Carlos Salsamendi, Tony Anderson, Martin_Jaggi, AMR Image, Asia Images Group, Liliboas, Elva Etienne, Adie Bush, Michaeljung, Gbh007, Izusek, Cindy Ord, Sisoje, Erik Isakson, Rbv, SerrNovik, Sean Justice, Ulrike Schmitt-Hartmann, Daniel Milchev, Alistair Berg, LSOphoto, Robert Niedring, The Good Brigade, Bharat Sanghavi, Fiordaliso, Forest_strider, Zoonar RF, Sergeyryzhov, Monty Rakusen, Flashpop, Daniel Boluda, Drazen_, Srdjan Radevic, JeanUrsula, Peter Muller, Tetra Images, Nick David, Chrisdorney, Manfred Gottschalk, Maskot, FotoVoyager, Loonger, Imgorthand, Sdominick, ER Productions Limited, Ozgurdonmaz, Jacobs Stock Photography Ltd, Mara Brandl, Russell Underwood, Luxy Images, Sam Edwards, Eric Anderson, Starcevic, ROMAOSLO, Paul Seheult, Alberto Clemares Exposito, FrankvandnBergh, Johrub, MaxOzerov, Matthias Rohrberg, 1st-ArtZone, Yongyuan, Sjo, franckreporter, AFP, Teoh Leog, Evemilla, BSANI, Manuel-F-O, Nkbimages, Pawel Libera, Denise Truscello, Susan.K., Batuhanozdel, Narvikk, Mitch Diamond, Bluejayphoto, Thomas Barwick, Annie Beauregard, Dusan Stankovic, TED ALJIBE, China Photos, Peter Adams, Miv123, OwenPrice, Stephanie Keenan, David Livingston, Kevin Mazur, RBL/Bauer-Griffin, Diego Fiore, Yorgil, Willie B.Thomas, Inaki Preysler, Artisteer, MilanEXPO, Djgunner, Jose A.Bernat Bacete, Karandaev, Edoma, Devonyu, Wavebreakmedia, Urbancow, Ozanuysal, Peter Griffith, Madodile, Belinda Howell, Photo And Co, Skynesher, Vincenzo Lombardo, David Malan, Scanrail, RENGraphic, Diane39, E71lena, Wragg, Hill Street Studios, Mr Nutnuchit Phutsawagung, HRAUN, Mint Images, Ewg3D, Highwaystarz-Photography, Goads Agency, Kaori Ando, Ray Kachatorian, Fizkes, Rick Neves, Buena Vista images, Kundoy, Laughingmango, Urbazon, Sylain Sonnet, Andresr; 123RF IMAGES/ Jaroslav Moravcik, Iakov Filimonov, dennizn; SWNS.

Cover Photo: GETTY IMAGES SALES SPAIN/Kealan Biebesheimer/EyeEm

The Publisher has made every effort to trace the owner of copyright material; however, the Publisher will correct any involuntary omission at the earliest opportunity.

Printed in Brazil
Impressão e acabamento: A.S. Pereira Gráfica e Editora EIRELI
Lote: 796.381 Código: 290527911
2024